CHICKEN

soups | salads | stir-fries | curries | grills | roasts

**THE AUSTRALIAN
Women's Weekly**

CONTENTS

As we were planning the recipes for this book, we soon realised that a cook could prepare a meal starring chicken as its main ingredient seven days a week for a very long time without duplication or terminal boredom. Chicken dishes abound in practically every country's cuisine – and with good reason: this versatile, relatively inexpensive all-rounder tastes great in any language.

Pamela Clark
Food Director

WEEKNIGHTS

Fast-cooking cuts for quick and easy mid-week meals. Dinner is on the table in less than an hour.

PREPARATION TIME 15 MINUTES
COOKING TIME 30 MINUTES SERVES 4

thai red curry

*You'll need about half a bunch
of snake beans for this recipe.*

2 cups (400g) jasmine rice
2 tablespoons peanut oil
750g thigh fillets, chopped coarsely
1 large brown onion (200g), chopped coarsely
3 cloves garlic, crushed
2 tablespoons red curry paste
1 fresh long red chilli, halved lengthways,
  sliced thinly
1 teaspoon ground cumin
3 baby eggplants (180g), sliced thickly
1 tablespoon fish sauce
3 fresh kaffir lime leaves, sliced thinly
140ml can coconut milk
¾ cup (180ml) water
150g snake beans, cut into 5cm lengths
⅓ cup loosely packed fresh coriander leaves

1 Cook rice in large saucepan of boiling water, uncovered, until just tender; drain.
2 Meanwhile, heat half of the oil in wok; stir-fry chicken, in batches, until browned.
3 Heat remaining oil in same wok; stir-fry onion and garlic until onion softens. Add paste, chilli and cumin; stir-fry until fragrant. Add eggplant; stir-fry until browned lightly.
4 Return chicken to wok with sauce, leaves, coconut milk, the water and beans; stir-fry about 5 minutes or until chicken is cooked through and sauce is thickened slightly.
5 Serve curry and rice sprinkled with coriander, and lime wedges, if desired.
per serving 34.4g total fat (12.6g saturated fat); 3557kJ (851 cal); 86.8g carbohydrate; 46g protein; 6g fibre

sticky drumettes with roasted root vegies

PREPARATION TIME 10 MINUTES
COOKING TIME 35 MINUTES SERVES 4

1   Preheat oven to hot (220°C/200°C fan-forced).

2   Combine vegetables, oil, rosemary and garlic in large shallow baking dish. Roast, uncovered, in single layer, about 35 minutes or until vegetables are just tender.

3   Meanwhile, combine paprika, salt, sugar, spices and syrup in large bowl; add drumettes, turn to coat in mixture. Place drumettes, in single layer, on oiled wire rack in large shallow baking dish; roast, uncovered, with vegetables about 30 minutes or until cooked through.

4   Serve drumettes with roasted vegetables.

per serving 30.5g total fat (7.7g saturated fat); 2483kJ (594 cal); 40g carbohydrate; 38.2g protein; 4.9g fibre

1 medium kumara (400g), cut into wedges
300g kipfler potatoes, cut into wedges
1 large parsnip (350g), cut into wedges
2 tablespoons olive oil
1 tablespoon coarsely chopped
   fresh rosemary
3 cloves garlic, crushed
1½ teaspoons sweet paprika
1 tablespoon coarse cooking salt
2 teaspoons caster sugar
½ teaspoon ground black pepper
½ teaspoon ground lemon myrtle
¼ teaspoon ground cinnamon
2 tablespoons maple syrup
20 drumettes (1.4kg)

smoked chicken salad with wild rice

PREPARATION TIME 10 MINUTES
COOKING TIME 15 MINUTES SERVES 6

2 cups (400g) wild rice blend
200g seedless red grapes
3 trimmed celery stalks (300g), sliced thinly
½ cup (60g) toasted pecans
350g watercress, trimmed
500g smoked chicken breasts, sliced thinly

LIME AND BLACK PEPPER DRESSING
½ cup (125ml) lime juice
½ cup (125ml) olive oil
1 tablespoon caster sugar
¼ teaspoon cracked black pepper

1 Cook rice in large saucepan of boiling water, uncovered, until just tender; drain. Rinse under cold water; drain.
2 Meanwhile, combine ingredients for lime and black pepper dressing in screw-top jar; shake well.
3 Place rice in large bowl with grapes, celery, nuts and half of the dressing; toss gently to combine.
4 Divide watercress among serving plates; top with rice salad then chicken. Drizzle with remaining dressing.
per serving 33.9g total fat (5.1g saturated fat); 2851kJ (682 cal); 61.9g carbohydrate; 29.1g protein; 6.4g fibre

The wild rice blend we use here is a packaged mixture of white long-grain and dark brown wild rice. The latter is the seed of a North American aquatic grass, which has a distinctively nutty flavour and a crunchy, resilient texture.

turkey steaks with mustard cream sauce on bacon mash

PREPARATION TIME 15 MINUTES
COOKING TIME 30 MINUTES SERVES 4

1 Make chive and bacon mash.

2 Melt half of the butter in large frying pan; cook steaks, in batches, until browned both sides.

3 Melt remaining butter in same pan; cook shallot and garlic, stirring, until soft. Add wine; bring to a boil. Reduce heat; simmer, uncovered, about 5 minutes or until almost evaporated. Stir in cream and mustard then return steaks to pan; bring to a boil. Reduce heat; simmer, covered, about 10 minutes or until steaks are cooked through.

4 Serve steaks with chive and bacon mash, drizzled with sauce.
BACON MASH Boil, steam or microwave potato until tender; drain. Cook bacon in small frying pan; drain on absorbent paper. Mash potato in large bowl with butter and cream until smooth. Stir in bacon and chives.

per serving 37.4g total fat (21.1g saturated fat); 2918kJ (698 cal); 30.8g carbohydrate; 52.3g protein; 3.8g fibre

20g butter
8 turkey steaks (880g)
2 shallots (50g), chopped finely
1 clove garlic, crushed
½ cup (125ml) dry white wine
½ cup (125ml) cream
2 teaspoons wholegrain mustard

BACON MASH
1kg medium potatoes, chopped coarsely
2 bacon rashers (140g), rind removed, chopped coarsely
20g butter
¼ cup (60ml) cream
1 tablespoon coarsely chopped fresh chives

Try using a dijon mustard with green peppercorns instead of wholegrain the next time you make this recipe – with the wine and the cream, it's a match made in culinary heaven.

PREPARATION TIME 15 MINUTES
COOKING TIME 40 MINUTES SERVES 4

chicken chowder

2 cups (500ml) chicken stock
2 cups (500ml) water
2 breast fillets (400g)
40g butter
2 bacon rashers (140g), rind removed,
  chopped coarsely
1 medium brown onion (150g), chopped finely
1 clove garlic, crushed
1 medium leek (350g), sliced thinly
1 trimmed celery stalk (100g), chopped finely
¼ cup (35g) plain flour
2 medium potatoes (400g), chopped coarsely
1 litre (4 cups) milk
½ cup (125ml) cream
2 tablespoons finely chopped fresh chives

1   Bring stock and the water to a boil in medium saucepan; add chicken, return to a boil. Reduce heat; simmer, covered, about 10 minutes or until chicken is cooked through. Cool chicken in poaching liquid 10 minutes. Remove chicken from pan; discard poaching liquid (or keep for another use). Shred chicken coarsely.
2   Meanwhile, heat butter in large saucepan; cook bacon, onion, garlic, leek and celery, stirring, until vegetables soften.
3   Stir in flour; cook, stirring, 1 minute. Stir in potato, milk and cream; simmer, covered, about 15 minutes or until potato is just tender.
4   Add chicken and chives: cook, stirring, until heated through.
per serving 37.3g total fat (22.6g saturated fat); 2721kJ (651 cal); 36.1g carbohydrate; 41.7g protein; 4.6g fibre

fettuccine alla pizzaiola

PREPARATION TIME 20 MINUTES
COOKING TIME 40 MINUTES SERVES 4

1   Preheat oven to moderately hot (200°C/180°C fan-forced).
2   Heat half of the oil in medium frying pan; cook garlic, stirring, over low heat, until fragrant. Add wine and stock; bring to a boil. Reduce heat; simmer, uncovered, 3 minutes. Add undrained tomatoes, oregano and parsley; bring to a boil. Reduce heat; simmer, uncovered, about 10 minutes or until pizzaiola sauce thickens slightly. Stir in olives.
3   Meanwhile, toss chicken in flour; shake away excess. Dip chicken fillets, one at a time, in combined eggs and milk, then breadcrumbs. Heat remaining oil in large frying pan; cook chicken, in batches, until browned lightly.
4   Place chicken, in single layer, in medium shallow baking dish; top with prosciutto, then pizzaiola sauce and finally cheese. Cook, uncovered, in oven about 20 minutes or until chicken is cooked through.
5   Meanwhile, cook pasta in large saucepan of boiling water, uncovered, until just tender; drain. Serve pasta topped with chicken pizzaiola.
per serving 42.4g total fat (13g saturated fat); 3821kJ (914 cal); 72g carbohydrate; 52.9g protein; 6.1g fibre

⅓ cup (80ml) olive oil
2 cloves garlic, crushed
½ cup (125ml) dry white wine
½ cup (125ml) chicken stock
2 x 400g cans crushed tomatoes
2 tablespoons coarsely chopped fresh oregano
2 tablespoons coarsely chopped fresh flat-leaf parsley
½ cup (75g) seeded kalamata olives
4 thigh fillets (440g)
¼ cup (35g) plain flour
2 eggs
1 tablespoon milk
1 cup (70g) stale breadcrumbs
7 slices prosciutto (110g)
1¾ cups (175g) grated mozzarella
250g fettuccine

Fettuccine comes from the Italian word "fettucina", meaning ribbon, because of its long, narrow shape. It goes especially well with creamy sauces; you can replace it with tagliatelli or other large egg noodles, if desired.

salad of greens, chicken livers, bacon and apple

PREPARATION TIME 15 MINUTES
COOKING TIME 15 MINUTES SERVES 4

4 bacon rashers (280g), rind removed,
  sliced thinly
1 tablespoon olive oil
500g chicken livers, halved, trimmed
200g lamb's lettuce
250g baby spinach leaves
1 medium apple (150g), halved,
  sliced into thin wedges

CRANBERRY DRESSING
4 shallots (100g), chopped finely
2 tablespoons red wine vinegar
⅓ cup (80ml) olive oil
¼ cup (80g) whole berry cranberry sauce, warmed

1   Combine ingredients for cranberry dressing in small bowl.
2   Cook bacon, stirring, in large frying pan until crisp; drain on absorbent paper.
3   Heat oil in same clean pan; cook liver, over high heat, about 5 minutes or until browned and cooked as desired (do not overcook or liver will be dry and tasteless). Drain on absorbent paper.
4   Place bacon, liver, lettuce, leaves, apple and dressing in large bowl; toss gently to combine.
per serving 33g total fat (6.7g saturated fat); 2027kJ (485 cal); 14.3g carbohydrate; 32.2g protein; 3.5g fibre

Lamb's lettuce, also known as mâche or corn salad, has a mild, almost nutty flavour and dark green leaves. It is usually sold in 125g punnets, but the leaves probably weigh only about a quarter of that total.

larb with thai pickle

PREPARATION TIME 15 MINUTES
COOKING TIME 15 MINUTES
(PLUS STANDING TIME) SERVES 4

1   Make thai pickle.

2   Meanwhile, place stock, juice, sauce and palm sugar in large saucepan; bring to a boil. Add chicken and garlic, reduce heat; simmer, stirring, about 5 minutes or until chicken is cooked through. Cool 10 minutes. Stir in shallot, herbs and chilli.

3   Serve larb with drained thai pickle on lettuce, accompanied with steamed jasmine rice, if desired.

THAI PICKLE Place sugar, vinegar, salt and the water in small saucepan; bring to a boil. Cool 5 minutes. Place capsicum, sprouts and cucumber in medium bowl; pour vinegar mixture over capsicum mixture. Cover; stand 30 minutes.

per serving 10.5g total fat (3.1g saturated fat); 1438kJ (344 cal); 34.1g carbohydrate; 26.7g protein; 2.9g fibre

¼ cup (60ml) chicken stock

2 tablespoons lime juice

1 tablespoon fish sauce

1 tablespoon grated palm sugar

500g mince

1 clove garlic, crushed

2 shallots (50g), sliced thinly

2 tablespoons finely chopped fresh coriander

1 tablespoon finely chopped fresh mint

1 fresh long red chilli, sliced thinly

1 medium iceberg lettuce, shredded coarsely

THAI PICKLE

½ cup (110g) white sugar

½ cup (125ml) white vinegar

1 tablespoon coarse cooking salt

½ cup (125ml) water

1 small red capsicum (150g), sliced thinly

½ cup (40g) bean sprouts

1 lebanese cucumber (130g), seeded, sliced thinly

Palm sugar, also called jaggery, jawa or gula melaka, is made from the sap of the sugar palm tree. Creamy to dark brown in colour and usually sold in rock-hard cakes; substitute brown sugar if it is unavailable.

turkish pilaf with chicken, onion and almonds

PREPARATION TIME 15 MINUTES
COOKING TIME 40 MINUTES SERVES 4

Chicken strips, called chicken stroganoff, are occasionally found in some poultry shops and supermarkets. If unavailable, make them by cutting breasts or thigh fillets into strips.

60g butter
500g strips
1 large brown onion (200g), sliced thinly
4 cloves garlic, crushed
⅓ cup (45g) slivered almonds
1 teaspoon ground allspice
½ teaspoon ground cinnamon
3 drained anchovies, chopped coarsely
2 tablespoons dried currants
1½ cups (300g) basmati rice
2 cups (500ml) chicken stock
1 cup (250ml) water
1 fresh long red chilli, chopped finely

1 Melt a third of the butter in large saucepan; cook chicken, in batches, until just cooked through.
2 Melt remaining butter in same pan; cook onion, garlic and nuts, stirring, until onion softens. Add spices, anchovies and currants; cook, stirring, 2 minutes. Add rice; cook, stirring, 2 minutes. Add stock and the water; bring to a boil. Reduce heat; simmer, covered tightly, 20 minutes or until rice is just tender.
3 Stir chicken into pilaf mixture; cook, covered, until heated through. Serve pilaf sprinkled with chilli, and parsley, if desired.
per serving 25.1g total fat (10.4g saturated fat); 2696kJ (645 cal); 67g carbohydrate; 36.5g protein; 3.3g fibre

Currants, named after the city of Corinth in Greece, are tiny, almost black raisins. They are commonly used in jams, jellies and sauces (the best-known of these being English Cumberland sauce). These are not the same as fresh currants, which are members of the gooseberry family.

salt and sichuan pepper drumettes with chilli and herb salad

PREPARATION TIME 20 MINUTES
COOKING TIME 35 MINUTES SERVES 4

1 Place stock, star anise and sauce in large saucepan; bring to a boil. Add drumettes, return to a boil then reduce heat; simmer, uncovered, about 20 minutes or until cooked through, turning drumettes occasionally. Drain; discard cooking liquid.

2 Combine ingredients for chilli and herb salad in medium bowl.

3 Heat oil in large saucepan. Toss drumettes in combined pepper, salt and flour; shake away excess. Deep-fry drumettes, in batches, until browned; drain on absorbent paper.

4 Serve drumettes with chilli and herb salad and lemon wedges.

per serving 32.4g total fat (8.6g saturated fat); 2006kJ (480 cal); 7.5g carbohydrate; 37.8g protein; 3.1g fibre

2 cups (500ml) chicken stock
1 star anise
2 tablespoons soy sauce
20 drumettes (1.4kg)
peanut oil, for deep-frying
2 teaspoons sichuan peppercorns, crushed coarsely
2 teaspoons coarse cooking salt
2 tablespoons plain flour
1 medium lemon (140g), cut into wedges

CHILLI AND HERB SALAD
1 cup coarsely chopped fresh garlic chives
1 cup loosely packed fresh mint leaves
1 fresh long red chilli, sliced thinly
2 tablespoons lemon juice
1½ cups (120g) bean sprouts

Sichuan peppercorns, also known as szechuan or chinese pepper, are a mild spice that comes from the prickly ash tree. They look like black peppercorns and have a distinctive peppery lemon flavour and aroma.

udon noodle soup

1.5 litres (6 cups) dashi
2 tablespoons japanese soy sauce
1 tablespoon mirin
2 teaspoons white sugar
2 breast fillets (400g)
100g fresh shiitake mushrooms, sliced thinly
300g dried udon noodles
230g can sliced bamboo shoots, rinsed, drained
8 large spinach leaves
4 eggs
4 green onions, sliced thinly

1 Preheat oven to hot (220°C/200°C fan-forced).
2 Bring dashi, sauce, mirin and sugar to a boil in large saucepan; add chicken and mushrooms, return to a boil. Reduce heat; simmer, uncovered, about 10 minutes or until chicken is cooked through. Cool chicken and mushrooms in cooking liquid 10 minutes. Remove chicken from pan, slice thinly. Reserve mushrooms and dashi broth.
3 Meanwhile, cook noodles in large saucepan of boiling water, uncovered, until just tender; drain. Rinse under cold water; drain.
4 Return broth to a boil. Divide noodles, chicken, bamboo shoots, spinach and hot broth with mushrooms among four 3-cup (750ml) ovenproof dishes. Make small hollows among noodles in each dish; break 1 egg into each hollow. Cook, uncovered, in oven about 10 minutes or until egg just sets.
5 Serve soup sprinkled with onion.
per serving 39g total fat (8.4g saturated fat); 4761kJ (1139 cal); 121.1g carbohydrate; 85.3g protein; 27.8g fibre

Dashi is the basic stock used in nearly every Japanese dish, from a spoonful or two in dipping sauces to greater amounts in the broths of one-pan dishes, such as the one we've made here.
The most common dashi, a combination of both kelp and smoked, dried bonito (tuna) flakes, is available in concentrated liquid as well as in granule or powdered form.
Make sure that the spinach leaves you use here are, in fact, true spinach, and not the coarser silver beet that is often sold as spinach.

pollo parmigiana-style

PREPARATION TIME 10 MINUTES
COOKING TIME 20 MINUTES SERVES 4

1 Preheat grill.
2 Split chicken fillets in half horizontally. Toss chicken in flour; shake away excess. Dip chicken pieces, one at a time, in combined egg and milk, then in breadcrumbs.
3 Heat oil in large frying pan; shallow-fry chicken, in batches, until browned and cooked through. Drain on absorbent paper.
4 Place chicken on oven tray; divide pasta sauce, then ham and finally cheese over chicken. Place under grill until cheese melts.
5 Serve with a parmesan and baby rocket salad, if desired.
per serving 28.6g total fat (8.7g saturated fat); 2103kJ (503 cal); 17.9g carbohydrate; 43.3g protein; 1.3g fibre

2 breast fillets (400g)
2 tablespoons plain flour
1 egg
1 tablespoon milk
1 cup (70g) stale breadcrumbs
¼ cup (60ml) vegetable oil
⅓ cup (85g) bottled tomato pasta
   sauce, warmed
4 slices leg ham (185g)
100g gruyère, grated coarsely

Gruyère, a firm, pale yellow, cows-milk cheese from the Fribourg canton in Switzerland, is also produced in many regions of France. It has a sweet, nutty taste and is delicious fresh or cooked. Substitute raclette, appenzeller or thurgaeur, if unavailable.

chicken, pea and broad bean risotto

PREPARATION TIME 15 MINUTES
COOKING TIME 40 MINUTES SERVES 4

1   Place stock and the water in medium saucepan; bring to a boil. Reduce heat; simmer, covered.

2   Heat half of the butter in large saucepan; cook chicken, in batches, until just browned.

3   Heat remaining butter in same pan; cook onion and garlic, stirring, until soft. Add rice; stir to coat in onion mixture. Add ½ cup of the simmering stock mixture; cook, stirring, over low heat until stock is absorbed. Continue adding stock, in ½-cup batches, stirring, until stock is absorbed after each addition. Return chicken to pan halfway through cooking time. Total cooking time should be about 35 minutes or until rice is tender.

4   Meanwhile, pour boiling water over beans; stand 2 minutes. Drain; peel away grey-coloured outer shells.

5   Add peas and beans to risotto, stir gently until hot. Remove from heat; stir in cheese and mint. Serve immediately, with a mixed leaf, parsley and mint salad, if desired.

per serving 24.7g total fat (13.3g saturated fat); 2951kJ (706 cal); 67.3g carbohydrate; 50.5g protein; 5.9g fibre

1 litre (4 cups) chicken stock
1 cup (250ml) water
50g butter
600g tenderloins, sliced thickly
4 green onions, sliced thinly
1 clove garlic, crushed
1½ cups (300g) arborio rice
1 cup (150g) frozen broad beans, thawed
1 cup (120g) frozen peas, thawed
1 cup (80g) finely grated parmesan
1 tablespoon finely chopped fresh mint

Broad beans, also known as fava beans, can be eaten fresh, but only when they are very young because, as the beans age, the pods become tougher. If using fresh beans, they should be blanched before cooking.

chinese barbecued wings with fried rice

PREPARATION TIME 15 MINUTES

COOKING TIME 40 MINUTES SERVES 4

10 large wings (1.2kg)

2 tablespoons honey

2 tablespoons soy sauce

2 fresh red thai chillies, chopped finely

FRIED RICE

1 tablespoon peanut oil

2 eggs, beaten lightly

4 bacon rashers (280g), rind removed,
    chopped coarsely

3 green onions, sliced thinly

½ cup (60g) frozen peas

½ cup (80g) frozen corn kernels

1 tablespoon soy sauce

3 cups cold cooked rice

1   Preheat oven to moderately hot (200°C/180°C fan-forced).

2   Cut wings into three pieces at joints; discard wing tips. Combine honey, sauce and chilli in large bowl; add wings, turn to coat in mixture.

3   Place undrained wings, in single layer, on oiled wire rack in large shallow baking dish; reserve any marinade in bowl. Roast, uncovered, brushing wings with marinade occasionally, about 40 minutes or until browned and cooked through, turning halfway through cooking time.

4   Meanwhile, make fried rice.

5   Serve wings with fried rice.

FRIED RICE Heat half of the oil in wok; cook egg over medium heat, swirling wok to form thin omelette. Remove from pan; cool. Roll omelette, cut into thin slices. Heat remaining oil in same wok; stir-fry bacon until crisp. Add onions, peas, corn, sauce, rice and omelette slices; stir-fry until hot.

per serving 23.1g total fat (6.9g saturated fat); 2876kJ (688 cal); 57.2g carbohydrate; 61.3g protein; 2.8g fibre

You need to cook 1½ cups (300g) white long-grain rice the day before making this recipe. Spread cooled cooked rice on a tray, cover; refrigerate overnight.

chicken, mushroom and asparagus creamy pasta bake

PREPARATION TIME 20 MINUTES
COOKING TIME 30 MINUTES **SERVES** 4

1   Preheat oven to moderately hot (200°C/180°C fan-forced).
2   Cook pasta in large saucepan of boiling water, uncovered, until just tender; drain.
3   Meanwhile, heat a third of the butter in large frying pan; cook chicken, in batches, until browned and cooked through.
4   Heat remaining butter in same pan; cook mushrooms, stirring, until tender. Add flour; cook, stirring, 1 minute. Gradually stir in milk. Stir over medium heat until mixture boils and thickens. Stir in chicken, ¼ cup of the romano, ¾ cup of the cheddar and the asparagus.
5   Combine chicken mixture and drained pasta in 2.5 litre (10-cup) ovenproof dish; sprinkle with remaining cheeses. Cook, uncovered, in oven about 15 minutes or until top browns lightly. Serve pasta bake sprinkled with parsley, and a mixed green salad, if desired.
per serving 37.3g total fat (22.3g saturated fat); 3775kJ (903 cal); 75.2g carbohydrate; 64g protein; 4.8g fibre

375g rigatoni
60g butter
600g breast fillets, diced into 1cm pieces
100g button mushrooms, sliced thinly
2 tablespoons plain flour
2 cups (500ml) milk
½ cup (40g) coarsely grated romano cheese
1¼ cups (150g) coarsely grated cheddar
170g asparagus, trimmed, chopped coarsely
¼ cup coarsely chopped fresh flat-leaf parsley

Rigatoni, a tube-shaped pasta with ridges on the outside, is an ideal pasta for "pasta al forno" (baked dishes) because it is wide and the hearty fillings cling to the indentations around the edges.

PREPARATION TIME 15 MINUTES
COOKING TIME 10 MINUTES SERVES 4

singapore noodles

450g fresh singapore noodles

2 teaspoons sesame oil

2 cloves garlic, crushed

2cm piece fresh ginger (10g), grated

1 medium carrot (120g), cut into matchsticks

250g cooked shelled small prawns

1 tablespoon malaysian curry powder

3 green onions, sliced thinly

1½ cups bean sprouts (120g)

2 tablespoons soy sauce

¼ cup (60ml) kecap manis

3 cups (480g) shredded barbecued chicken

1 Place noodles in large heatproof bowl; cover with boiling water. Separate noodles with fork; drain.

2 Meanwhile, heat oil in wok; stir-fry garlic, ginger and carrot until carrot is just tender. Add prawns and curry powder; stir-fry until prawns change colour.

3 Add noodles and remaining ingredients; stir-fry until hot.

per serving 19.1g total fat (6.4g saturated fat); 2057kJ (492 cal); 27.3g carbohydrate; 49.1g protein; 5.8g fibre

You need to purchase a large barbecued chicken weighing approximately 900g to get the amount of shredded meat required for this recipe.

quesadillas with guacamole

PREPARATION TIME 15 MINUTES
COOKING TIME 30 MINUTES SERVES 4

1   Heat oil in large frying pan; cook garlic and onion, stirring, until onion softens. Add spices and capsicums; cook, stirring, until capsicums soften. Remove from heat; stir in chicken.

2   Place one tortilla on board; top with ¼ cup of the cheese, then a quarter of the chicken mixture and finally another ¼ cup of the cheese. Top with a second tortilla. Repeat with remaining tortillas, cheese and chicken mixture.

3   Cook quesadillas, one at a time, uncovered, in same large lightly oiled frying pan, over medium heat, until golden brown. Turn quesadilla, browned-side up, onto large plate then carefully slide back into pan, uncooked-side down. Remove from pan when golden brown both sides; cover to keep warm while cooking remaining quesadillas.

4   Meanwhile, place guacamole ingredients in medium bowl; mash with fork to combine.

5   Serve quesadillas, cut into quarters, with guacamole and, if desired, a dollop of sour cream and a little shredded iceberg lettuce.

per serving 66g total fat (22.7g saturated fat); 4393kJ (1051 cal); 54.3g carbohydrate; 57.1g protein; 6.5g fibre

1 tablespoon olive oil
2 cloves garlic, crushed
1 small red onion (100g), chopped finely
¼ teaspoon cayenne pepper
2 teaspoons ground cumin
1 medium red capsicum (200g), chopped finely
1 medium green capsicum (200g), chopped finely
3 cups (480g) shredded barbecued chicken
8 large flour tortillas
2 cups (240g) coarsely grated cheddar

GUACAMOLE
1 tablespoon finely chopped fresh coriander
1 large tomato (220g), seeded, chopped finely
½ small red onion (50g), chopped finely
2 large avocados (640g), chopped coarsely
2 tablespoons lime juice

Quesadillas are flour tortillas enclosing a savoury filling, and are grilled or fried before being served. You need to purchase a large barbecued chicken weighing approximately 900g to get the amount of shredded meat required for this recipe.

chicken, mushroom and fennel pies with rocket salad

PREPARATION TIME 20 MINUTES

COOKING TIME 30 MINUTES SERVES 4

1 tablespoon olive oil

2 cloves garlic, crushed

1 medium leek (350g), sliced thinly

1 small fennel bulb (200g), sliced thinly

200g button mushrooms, quartered

½ cup (125ml) dry white wine

4 breast fillets (800g), chopped coarsely

300ml cream

1 tablespoon dijon mustard

¼ cup coarsely chopped fresh flat-leaf parsley

1 sheet puff pastry, cut into quarters

1 egg, beaten lightly

1 tablespoon fennel seeds

1 Preheat oven to moderately hot (200°C/180°C fan-forced).

2 Heat oil in large saucepan; cook garlic, leek, fennel and mushrooms, stirring, until vegetables soften.

3 Stir in wine; bring to a boil. Reduce heat; simmer, uncovered, 3 minutes. Add chicken and cream; bring to a boil. Reduce heat; simmer, uncovered, about 10 minutes or until chicken is cooked through and sauce thickened slightly. Stir in mustard and parsley.

4 Meanwhile, place pastry quarters onto oven tray, brush pastry with egg then sprinkle with seeds; bake in oven about 10 minutes or until golden brown.

5 Divide chicken mixture among small serving bowls, top each with pastry; serve with rocket salad.

per serving 52.8g total fat (28.8g saturated fat); 3340kJ (799 cal); 20.9g carbohydrate; 54g protein; 4.4g fibre

These pies taste wonderful with a fresh rocket salad dressed with 2 tablespoons lime juice, a tablespoon of olive oil and a clove of garlic. Combine this with 100g baby rocket leaves, ¼ cup coarsely chopped fresh flat-leaf parsley and ¼ cup fresh mint leaves. Sprinkle with 2 chopped green onions.

chicken caesar salad

PREPARATION TIME 5 MINUTES
COOKING TIME 20 MINUTES SERVES 4

1   Preheat oven to moderate (180°C/160°C fan-forced).
2   Make caesar dressing by blending or processing ingredients until mixture is smooth.
3   Remove crusts from bread; discard crusts, cut bread into 2cm squares; toss with oil in medium bowl. Place bread, in single layer, on oven tray; toast in oven, 10 minutes.
4   Cook bacon in small frying pan, stirring, until browned and crisp. Drain on absorbent paper.
5   Combine half of the chicken, half of the bacon, half of the croutons and half of the dressing in large bowl with lettuce, half of the onion and half of the cheese; toss to combine.
6   Divide salad among serving plates. Top with remaining chicken, bacon, croutons, onion and cheese; drizzle with remaining dressing.
per serving 49.9g total fat (12.3g saturated fat); 3390kJ (811 cal); 35.6g carbohydrate; 52.6g protein; 6.3g fibre

4 slices white bread (180g)
2 tablespoons olive oil
4 bacon rashers (280g), rind removed, sliced thinly
3 cups (480g) coarsely chopped barbecued chicken
1 large cos lettuce, trimmed, torn
6 green onions, sliced thinly
1 cup (80g) flaked parmesan

CAESAR DRESSING
¾ cup (225g) whole-egg mayonnaise
1 tablespoon lemon juice
4 drained anchovy fillets, chopped finely
3 teaspoons dijon mustard
1 tablespoon water

Crouton, a French word meaning "little crust", is a small cube of toasted or fried bread usually used to garnish soups or salads. They are a fantastic way to use up yesterday's bread. For a twist, add some garlic or herbs when making your croutons.

You need to purchase a large barbecued chicken weighing approximately 900g to get the amount of chopped meat required for this recipe.

farfalle with tenderloins, ricotta, spinach and tomato

PREPARATION TIME 15 MINUTES
COOKING TIME 10 MINUTES SERVES 4

375g farfalle
1 tablespoon olive oil
1 medium brown onion (150g), chopped finely
1 clove garlic, crushed
600g tenderloins, chopped coarsely
150g baby spinach leaves
1 cup (200g) ricotta
1 egg
2 teaspoons finely grated lemon rind
2 tablespoons lemon juice
200g grape tomatoes, halved
¼ cup (20g) finely grated parmesan

1 Cook pasta in large saucepan of boiling water, uncovered, until just tender; drain.
2 Meanwhile, heat oil in large deep frying pan; cook onion and garlic, stirring, until onion softens. Add chicken; cook, stirring, over medium heat, about 5 minutes or until cooked through.
3 Place chicken mixture, spinach, combined ricotta and egg, rind, juice, tomato and drained pasta in large serving bowl; toss gently to combine.
4 Serve sprinkled with grated parmesan.

per serving 20.7g total fat (7.7g saturated fat); 2851kJ (682 cal); 67.7g carbohydrate; 52.2g protein; 5.6g fibre

Farfalle are a short, rather sturdy, butterfly-shaped pasta that some people refer to as bow ties. They are good used in dishes such as this one because they help hold the other ingredients. You can replace the farfalle with penne or shells, if you like.

asian burgers

PREPARATION TIME 15 MINUTES
COOKING TIME 25 MINUTES SERVES 4

1 Preheat grill.

2 Heat oil in small frying pan; cook lemon grass and onion, stirring, until onion softens. Add five-spice, chilli, sauce, rind and coconut cream; bring to a boil. Boil sauce mixture, uncovered, until reduced by half; cool 5 minutes.

3 Combine half of the sauce with peanut butter in small bowl. Combine remaining sauce with chicken, breadcrumbs, coriander and egg in large bowl; use hands to shape chicken mixture into four patties.

4 Using vegetable peeler; slice carrot and cucumber into thin strips.

5 Cook patties in heated lightly oiled large frying pan, uncovered, about 15 minutes or until cooked through.

6 Meanwhile, halve buns horizontally; toast, cut-sides up, under preheated grill. Spread peanut butter mixture on bun tops; sandwich patties, carrot and cucumber between bun halves.

per serving 29.5g total fat (11.5g saturated fat); 2746kJ (657 cal); 54.9g carbohydrate; 39.7g protein; 7g fibre

1 teaspoon peanut oil
10cm stick (20g) finely chopped
  fresh lemon grass
1 small red onion (100g), chopped finely
½ teaspoon five-spice powder
½ teaspoon dried chilli flakes
1 tablespoon fish sauce
2 teaspoons finely grated lime rind
140ml can coconut cream
2 tablespoons crunchy peanut butter
500g mince
1 cup (70g) stale breadcrumbs
¼ cup finely chopped fresh coriander
1 egg
1 medium carrot (120g)
1 lebanese cucumber (130g)
4 hamburger buns

A new style of grater, known as a microplane, has taken the foodie market by storm. Its design resembles a small metal cricket bat covered in tiny razor-like holes along its length. It is very easy and fast to use, and provides a fine, almost fluffy, shaved grate; it can also be used to grate chocolate, cheese, garlic, ginger and nutmeg. The traditional small grater usually costs just a few dollars, while the newer, bigger grater costs around $40; however, for a keen cook, it's worth the price.

crumbed schnitzel with mixed bean salad

PREPARATION TIME 25 MINUTES
COOKING TIME 20 MINUTES SERVES 4

300g green beans
200g yellow beans
4 medium tomatoes (600g),
   seeded, sliced thickly
2 tablespoons olive oil
1 tablespoon red wine vinegar
2 teaspoons wholegrain mustard
2 tablespoons coarsely chopped fresh tarragon
2 tablespoons coarsely chopped fresh chervil
2 teaspoons drained green peppercorns, crushed
4 breast fillets (800g)
¼ cup (35g) plain flour
2 eggs, beaten lightly
1 tablespoon milk
2 teaspoons finely grated lemon rind
½ cup (85g) polenta
½ cup (50g) packaged breadcrumbs
vegetable oil, for shallow-frying

1   Boil, steam or microwave beans until tender. Rinse under cold water; drain. Place beans in large bowl with tomato, olive oil, vinegar, mustard, herbs and peppercorns; toss gently to combine. Cover; refrigerate until required.
2   Using meat mallet, gently pound chicken, one piece at a time, between sheets of plastic wrap until 1cm thick.
3   Whisk flour, egg, milk and rind together in shallow bowl; combine polenta and breadcrumbs in a second shallow bowl. Coat chicken pieces, first in egg mixture then in breadcrumb mixture.
4   Heat vegetable oil in large frying pan; shallow-fry chicken, in batches, until browned and cooked through. Drain on absorbent paper.
5   Serve schnitzel, sliced, with bean salad.
per serving 35.4g total fat (5.8g saturated fat); 2897kJ (693 cal); 33.5g carbohydrate; 57.1g protein; 5.8g fibre

Polenta, a staple in northern Italy, is the name given to both starchy cornmeal and the dish made from it. It can be eaten on its own, either just cooked or cut into slices and fried. Here we have used it to coat schnitzel, which gives the chicken a lovely thick texture and hearty flavour.

chicken sang choy bow

PREPARATION TIME 10 MINUTES

COOKING TIME 15 MINUTES SERVES 4

1   Heat oil in wok; stir-fry chilli and garlic until fragrant. Add chicken and capsicum; stir-fry until chicken is cooked through.

2   Add juice, nuts, basil, kecap manis and sprouts; stir-fry 1 minute. Stir in half of the noodles.

3   Divide sang choy bow among lettuce leaves; serve sprinkled with remaining noodles.

per serving 25.1g total fat (4.2g saturated fat); 1735kJ (415 cal);
16.2g carbohydrate; 28.3g protein, 5g fibre

1 tablespoon peanut oil

1 fresh long red chilli, chopped finely

2 cloves garlic, crushed

400g mince

1 small red capsicum (150g), chopped finely

⅓ cup (80ml) lemon juice

½ cup (80g) blanched almonds, toasted, chopped finely

½ cup finely chopped fresh basil

2 tablespoons kecap manis

1 cup (80g) bean sprouts

100g crisp fried noodles

12 iceberg lettuce leaves, crisped

For easy removal of lettuce leaves without any tearing, remove core from iceberg lettuce by holding lettuce core-end down, smash lettuce down on kitchen bench. This loosens the outer leaves, which will come away without tearing. Holding the cored end under a running cold water tap also forces the leaves to fall off intact. You need a large iceberg lettuce for this recipe. Fried noodles are sold in 100g packets in supermarkets and Asian food stores.

satay pizza with rocket and raita

PREPARATION TIME 20 MINUTES
COOKING TIME 15 MINUTES SERVES 4

½ cup (140g) crunchy peanut butter
½ cup (125ml) sweet chilli sauce
4 x 15cm prepared pizza bases
3 cups (480g) shredded barbecued chicken
200g provolone cheese, grated coarsely
50g baby rocket leaves

RAITA
1 lebanese cucumber (130g), chopped finely
1 small brown onion (80g), chopped finely
½ cup (140g) yogurt
2 tablespoons finely chopped fresh mint
1 long green chilli, chopped finely

1   Preheat oven to moderately hot (200°C/180°C fan-forced).
2   Combine peanut butter and chilli sauce in small bowl.
3   Place pizza bases on oven trays; spread sauce mixture evenly over each base. Divide chicken and cheese among bases; bake about 15 minutes or until pizza tops brown and bases crisp.
4   Meanwhile, combine raita ingredients in small bowl.
5   Serve pizza topped with raita and rocket.
per serving 48.1g total fat (16.3g saturated fat); 4301kJ (1029 cal); 73.1g carbohydrate; 70.5g protein; 10.6g fibre

Pre-baked, packaged pizza bases first appeared in supermarkets during the 1980s. They come in various sizes, some with cheese already in the mix.

You need to purchase a large barbecued chicken weighing approximately 900g to get the amount of shredded meat required for this recipe.

chilli-chicken stir-fry with asian greens

PREPARATION TIME 10 MINUTES
COOKING TIME 15 MINUTES SERVES 4

1   Cook rice in large saucepan of boiling water, uncovered, until just tender; drain. Cover to keep warm.

2   Heat half of the oil in wok; stir-fry chicken, in batches, until cooked through. Return chicken to wok with garlic, capsicum, jam, sauce and stock; stir-fry about 2 minutes or until sauce thickens slightly. Remove from wok.

3   Heat remaining oil in same cleaned wok; stir-fry bok choy, chestnuts and onion until bok choy just wilts. Divide bok choy mixture among serving plates; top with chilli chicken, sprinkle with sesame seeds. Serve with rice.

per serving 13.7g total fat (2.7g saturated fat); 3490kJ (835 cal); 115.9g carbohydrate; 57.6g protein; 5.4g fibre

2½ cups (500g) jasmine rice
1 tablespoon sesame oil
4 breast fillets (800g), sliced thinly
2 cloves garlic, crushed
1 large red capsicum (350g), sliced thinly
⅓ cup (100g) thai chilli jam
2 tablespoons sweet chilli sauce
¼ cup (60ml) chicken stock
500g baby bok choy, halved lengthways
225g can water chestnuts, drained, halved
4 green onions, sliced thinly
1 tablespoon sesame seeds, toasted

The mildly acidic baby bok choy, far smaller and more tender than bok choy, is perhaps the most popular of all the Asian greens that are so readily available year-round in supermarkets everywhere today. They should be refrigerated, airtight, no more than four days.

sumac-flavoured drumettes with tomato, rocket and herb salad

PREPARATION TIME 10 MINUTES
COOKING TIME 20 MINUTES SERVES 4

20 drumettes (1.4kg)
¼ cup (25g) sumac
¼ cup (60ml) olive oil
1 lebanese cucumber (130g), halved lengthways, sliced thickly
2 medium tomatoes (300g), chopped coarsely
1 medium green capsicum (200g), chopped finely
¾ cup coarsely chopped fresh flat-leaf parsley
¼ cup coarsely chopped fresh mint
50g baby rocket leaves
2 tablespoons lemon juice

1   Combine drumettes and sumac in large bowl.
2   Heat 2 tablespoons of the oil in large frying pan; cook drumettes, in batches, covered, turning occasionally until browned and cooked through.
3   Meanwhile, place remaining oil in large bowl with cucumber, tomato, capsicum, herbs, rocket and juice; toss gently to combine.
4   Serve drumettes with salad.
per serving 34.9g total fat (8.3g saturated fat); 1986kJ (475 cal); 3.8g carbohydrate; 35.6g protein; 2.4g fibre

A purple-red, astringent spice ground from berries growing on shrubs that flourish wild around the Mediterranean, sumac adds a tart, lemony flavour to dips and dressings and goes well with barbecued meat. It can be found in Middle Eastern food stores and major supermarkets.

grilled thigh fillets with salsa verde and kipfler smash

PREPARATION TIME 15 MINUTES
COOKING TIME 25 MINUTES SERVES 4

1   Combine ingredients for salsa verde in small bowl.

2   Place ⅓ cup of the salsa verde in medium bowl; add chicken, turn to coat in salsa marinade.

3   Cook chicken on heated oiled grill plate (or grill or barbecue) until browned both sides and cooked through.

4   Meanwhile, boil, steam or microwave potatoes until tender; drain. Using potato masher, crush potato roughly in large bowl with butter. Cover to keep warm.

5   Serve chicken with potato topped with remaining salsa verde.

per serving 45.3g total fat (14.3g saturated fat); 2897kJ (693 cal); 22.1g carbohydrate; 47.2g protein; 3.5g fibre

8 thigh fillets (880g)
600g kipfler potatoes, unpeeled
50g butter, chopped

SALSA VERDE
½ cup coarsely chopped fresh flat-leaf parsley
¼ cup coarsely chopped fresh mint
⅓ cup (80ml) olive oil
½ cup (125ml) lemon juice
¼ cup (50g) drained capers, chopped coarsely
8 anchovy fillets, drained, chopped finely
2 cloves garlic, crushed

We think salsa verde is just as good as pesto. It's not a spicy Mexican-type salsa but Italian, with a herbaceous, zesty, lemony flavour that goes well with fish and simple meat dishes. The herbs used in salsa verde can vary, with the single common denominator being parsley.

PREPARATION TIME 20 MINUTES
COOKING TIME 5 MINUTES SERVES 4

vietnamese duck salad

2 medium carrots (240g), cut into matchsticks
150g snow peas, sliced thinly
150g fresh baby corn, quartered lengthways
250g dried rice stick noodles
1kg chinese barbecued duck
1 cup (80g) bean sprouts
¼ cup coarsely chopped fresh vietnamese mint
¼ cup coarsely chopped fresh coriander
2 small red thai chillies, chopped finely

GINGER AND LEMON GRASS DRESSING
2cm piece fresh ginger (10g), grated
10cm stick (20g) finely chopped fresh lemon grass
2 tablespoons grated palm sugar
½ cup (125ml) lime juice
2 tablespoons fish sauce

1 Combine ingredients for ginger and lemon grass dressing in screw-top jar; shake well.
2 Plunge carrot, snow peas and corn in large saucepan of boiling water for 30 seconds; rinse immediately under cold water.
3 Cook noodles, uncovered, in large saucepan of boiling water until just tender; drain.
4 Remove and discard skin and bones from duck; slice meat thinly.
5 Place vegetables, noodles and duck in large bowl with sprouts, herbs, chilli and dressing; toss gently to combine.
per serving 38.1g total fat (11.1g saturated fat); 2587kJ (619 cal); 32g carbohydrate; 34.4g protein; 5.7g fibre

Rice stick noodles come in different widths: the thin ones are used in soups and the wide in stir-fries. Soak in hot water until soft. In this recipe the vegetables are blanched, meaning they are plunged briefly into boiling water then refreshed under cold water to soften them and intensify their colour.

turkey, avocado and cranberry wraps

PREPARATION TIME 10 MINUTES
COOKING TIME 25 MINUTES SERVES 4

1 Cut steaks in half horizontally.
2 Heat oil in large frying pan; cook steaks, in batches, until browned and cooked through. Stand 5 minutes; cut into thin strips.
3 Place turkey in large bowl with sauce, onion and juice; toss to combine.
4 Heat tortillas according to manufacturer's instructions.
5 Spread each tortilla with a quarter of each avocado. Divide turkey mixture, spinach and snow pea sprouts among tortillas; roll to enclose filling.

per serving 35.5g total fat (7.3g saturated fat); 3511kJ (840 cal); 71.4g carbohydrate; 56g protein; 6.2g fibre

800g turkey steaks
2 teaspoons olive oil
½ cup (160g) whole berry cranberry sauce
½ small red onion (50g), chopped finely
1 tablespoon lemon juice
8 large flour tortillas
2 medium avocados (500g)
100g baby spinach leaves
100g snow pea sprouts, trimmed

Cranberries are high in vitamin C and often used in sauces or jams as an accompaniment to traditional roast turkey. These tangy berries are also known as "bounceberries" because the ripe berries contain an air pocket which allows them to bounce.

WEEKENDS

A slower pace is necessary for the weekend – and there's no need to rush in the kitchen, either.

PREPARATION TIME 20 MINUTES
COOKING TIME 50 MINUTES SERVES 4

lebanese-spiced drumsticks with baba ghanoush

2 teaspoons ground allspice
1 teaspoon ground black pepper
1 teaspoon ground cumin
2 tablespoons olive oil
8 drumsticks (1.2kg)
4 large pittas

BABA GHANOUSH
2 medium eggplants (600g)
1 clove garlic, crushed
1 tablespoon tahini
¼ cup (60ml) lemon juice
2 tablespoons olive oil

1   Preheat oven to moderately hot (200°C/180°C fan-forced).
2   Make baba ghanoush.
3   Meanwhile, combine spices and oil in large bowl, add drumsticks; turn to coat in mixture.
4   Place drumsticks on wire rack over dish. Roast, uncovered, about 50 minutes or until chicken is cooked through, turning occasionally.
5   Serve drumsticks with baba ghanoush and bread, and lemon wedges and fresh parsley, if desired.
BABA GHANOUSH Pierce eggplants all over with fork; place on oiled oven tray. Roast, uncovered, about 40 minutes or until eggplant is soft, turning occasionally. Stand 10 minutes. Peel eggplant, discard skin; drain eggplant in colander 10 minutes then blend or process with garlic, tahini, juice and oil.
per serving 44.4g total fat (9.5g saturated fat); 3164kJ (757 cal);
43.6g carbohydrate; 43.2g protein; 6.2g fibre

ravioli with asian greens

PREPARATION TIME 40 MINUTES
COOKING TIME 30 MINUTES SERVES 4

1   Heat oil in wok; stir-fry onion, ginger and garlic until onion softens. Add mince; stir-fry until mince changes colour. Add soy sauce, five-spice and cabbage; stir-fry until cabbage is tender. Stir in coriander; cool 10 minutes.

2   Place 1 level tablespoon of the mince mixture in centre of one wrapper; brush around edges with water. Top with another wrapper; press edges together to seal. Repeat with remaining mince mixture and wrappers.

3   Add stock, the water, chilli, extra soy sauce, char siu sauce and wine to same cleaned wok; bring to a boil. Cook ravioli, in batches, uncovered, about 3 minutes or until ravioli float to surface. Using slotted spoon, remove ravioli; drain.

4   Cook bok choy and snow peas in stock mixture until vegetables are tender.

5   Divide ravioli and vegetables among serving bowls; ladle stock mixture over vegetables.

per serving 15.8g total fat (3.8g saturated fat); 2161kJ (517 cal); 52.9g carbohydrate; 35.9g protein; 4.3g fibre

1 tablespoon sesame oil
4 green onions, chopped finely
4cm piece fresh ginger (20g), grated
4 cloves garlic, crushed
450g mince
2 tablespoons soy sauce
½ teaspoon five-spice powder
100g chinese cabbage, sliced thinly
¼ cup coarsely chopped fresh coriander
40 wonton wrappers
1½ cups (375ml) chicken stock
1½ cups (375ml) water
2 fresh small red thai chillies, chopped finely
2 tablespoons soy sauce, extra
1 tablespoon char siu sauce
¼ cup (60ml) chinese cooking wine
500g baby bok choy, quartered lengthways
150g snow peas, trimmed, halved

PREPARATION TIME 40 MINUTES
COOKING TIME 1 HOUR 30 MINUTES
(PLUS COOLING TIME) SERVES 4

liver and asparagus terrine

12 slices prosciutto (180g)

¼ cup (60ml) olive oil

1 large brown onion (200g), chopped finely

4 cloves garlic, crushed

¼ cup (60ml) cream

250g mushrooms, sliced thinly

⅓ cup (25g) coarsely grated parmesan

400g chicken livers, halved, trimmed

700g mince

250g asparagus, trimmed

4 large potatoes (1.2 kg), chopped coarsely

CELERIAC COLESLAW

½ cup (150g) whole-egg mayonnaise

200g celeriac, grated coarsely

2 tablespoons dijon mustard

2 tablespoons lemon juice

1   Preheat oven to moderate (180°C/160°C fan-forced). Lightly oil 1.5-litre (6-cup) ovenproof terrine dish.

2   Line base and sides of dish with prosciutto slices, allowing 7cm overhang on long sides of dish.

3   Heat 1 tablespoon of the oil in large frying pan; cook onion and garlic, stirring, until onion softens. Stir in cream; transfer to medium bowl.

4   Heat 1 tablespoon of the remaining oil in same pan; cook mushrooms, stirring, until browned. Stir in cheese; transfer to another medium bowl.

5   Heat remaining oil in same pan; cook liver, stirring, over high heat, about 2 minutes or until browned, but not cooked through. Drain on absorbent paper.

6   Combine liver and mince with onion mixture in medium bowl. Spread one third of the mince mixture into dish; top with asparagus. Cover with another third of the mince mixture; top with mushroom mixture, then top with remaining mince mixture. Fold prosciutto slices over to cover mince mixture.

7   Roast, uncovered, in oven about 1 hour or until chicken is cooked through. Remove terrine from oven; drain juices from dish. Cool 20 minutes in dish before slicing.

8   Meanwhile, place potato on oiled oven tray. Roast, uncovered, alongside terrine, about 1 hour or until potato is tender and browned lightly.

9   Combine ingredients for celeriac coleslaw in medium bowl. Serve terrine with potato and coleslaw.

per serving 55.8g total fat (15.4g saturated fat); 4285kJ (1025 cal); 50.4g carbohydrate; 74.9g protein; 10.5g fibre

butter chicken
with onion sultana pilaf

PREPARATION TIME 20 MINUTES
(PLUS REFRIGERATION TIME)
COOKING TIME 1 HOUR SERVES 4

1   Dry-fry garam masala and chilli in small frying pan, stirring, until fragrant.

2   Blend or process chilli mixture with garlic, ginger, juice, paste, half of the nuts and half of the buttermilk until smooth. Combine nut mixture, remaining buttermilk and chicken in large bowl, cover; refrigerate 3 hours or overnight.

3   Melt butter in large saucepan; cook onion, cinnamon and cardamom, stirring, until onion browns. Add undrained chicken mixture; cook, uncovered, 10 minutes, stirring occasionally.

4   Add undrained tomatoes and stock; bring to a boil. Reduce heat; simmer, uncovered, stirring occasionally, about 35 minutes or until chicken is cooked through and mixture thickens slightly. Remove from heat; discard cinnamon. Stir in extra buttermilk.

5   Meanwhile make onion and sultana pilaf.

6   Coarsely chop remaining nuts.

7   Serve chicken with pilaf, topped with chopped nuts and coriander.
ONION SULTANA PILAF Melt butter in medium saucepan; cook onion and seeds, stirring, until onion browns lightly. Add rice; cook, stirring, 1 minute. Stir in stock and sultanas; bring to a boil. Reduce heat; simmer, covered tightly, about 25 minutes or until rice is just tender and liquid has been absorbed. Remove from heat; fluff rice with fork. Stand, covered, 5 minutes.

per serving 51.8g total fat (19.3g saturated fat); 4464kJ (1068 cal); 90.7g carbohydrate; 56.6g protein; 7.9g fibre

1 tablespoon garam masala
1 teaspoon chilli powder
2 cloves garlic, chopped coarsely
4cm piece fresh ginger (20g), grated
2 tablespoons lemon juice
⅓ cup (90g) tomato paste
1 cup (150g) roasted, unsalted cashews
¼ cup (60ml) buttermilk
800g thigh fillets, chopped coarsely
40g butter
1 large brown onion (200g), sliced thinly
1 cinnamon stick
6 cardamom pods, bruised
425g can crushed tomatoes
¾ cup (180ml) chicken stock
¼ cup (60ml) buttermilk, extra
¼ cup loosely packed fresh coriander leaves

ONION SULTANA PILAF
40g butter
2 medium brown onions (300g), sliced thinly
2 teaspoons yellow mustard seeds
1½ cups (300g) basmati rice
3 cups (750ml) chicken stock
⅓ cup (55g) sultanas

roasted spatchcock with dill and walnut pesto

⅓ cup firmly packed fresh flat-leaf parsley leaves
½ cup firmly packed fresh dill sprigs
½ cup (50g) toasted walnuts, chopped coarsely
¼ cup (20g) finely grated parmesan
¼ cup (60ml) lemon juice
¼ cup (60ml) olive oil
4 x 500g spatchcocks
2 medium lemons (280g), quartered

RISONI SALAD
1 cup (220g) risoni
6 slices pancetta (90g), chopped finely
⅓ cup (50g) toasted pine nuts
¼ cup finely chopped fresh basil
¼ cup finely chopped fresh flat-leaf parsley
2 tablespoons olive oil
1 tablespoon red wine vinegar

1 Preheat oven to moderate (180°C/160°C fan-forced).
2 Blend or process herbs, nuts, cheese and juice until combined. With motor operating, gradually add oil in thin, steady stream until pesto thickens slightly. Reserve 1 tablespoon of pesto for risoni salad.
3 Wash spatchcocks under cold water. Discard necks; pat dry inside and out with absorbent paper. Loosen spatchcock skin; rub remaining pesto between skin and flesh and over outside of spatchcocks. Place 2 lemon quarters in cavity of each spatchcock.
4 Place spatchcocks on oiled wire rack over baking dish; roast, uncovered, about 45 minutes or until cooked through.
5 Meanwhile, make risoni salad.
6 Remove spatchcocks from baking dish; discard pan juices. Halve spatchcocks lengthways; serve spatchcocks with salad.
per serving 85.1g total fat (18.9g saturated fat); 5029kJ (1203 cal); 40.3g carbohydrate; 65.5g protein; 5.5g fibre

RISONI SALAD Cook pasta in large saucepan of boiling water, uncovered, until just tender; drain. Cook pancetta in small heated non-stick frying pan, stirring, about 5 minutes or until crisp. Place pasta and pancetta in large bowl with nuts, herbs, oil, vinegar and reserved pesto; toss gently to combine.

chicken breast stuffed with smoked salmon and goat cheese

PREPARATION TIME 25 MINUTES
COOKING TIME 1 HOUR 15 MINUTES SERVES 4

1   Preheat oven to moderately hot (200°C/180°C fan-forced).

2   Combine potato, parsley, garlic and oil in medium bowl. Layer potato mixture in 2.5-litre (10-cup) ceramic baking dish; pour over milk. Roast, uncovered, about 40 minutes or until potato is just tender.

3   Meanwhile, combine chives and cheese in small bowl. Cut fillets in half horizontally almost all the way through; open out each fillet. Spread each fillet with a quarter of the cheese mixture; top with one slice of salmon and a quarter of the spinach. Roll each fillet tightly to enclose filling; secure with toothpicks.

4   Cook chicken in large oiled frying pan, uncovered, until browned.

5   Place chicken on cooked potato; roast, uncovered, in oven about 15 minutes or until chicken is cooked through. Stand 5 minutes; remove toothpicks, slice chicken thickly.

6   Meanwhile, place ingredients for spinach salad in medium bowl; toss gently to combine.

7   Serve chicken with potato and salad.

per serving 21g total fat (6.4g saturated fat); 2316kJ (554 cal); 26g carbohydrate; 62.1g protein; 4.4g fibre

4 medium potatoes (800g), sliced thinly
¼ cup coarsely chopped fresh flat-leaf parsley
2 cloves garlic, crushed
1 tablespoon olive oil
⅔ cup (160ml) milk, warmed
2 tablespoons finely chopped fresh chives
100g soft goat cheese
4 breast fillets (800g)
4 slices smoked salmon (120g)
50g baby spinach leaves

SPINACH SALAD

100g baby spinach leaves
1 tablespoon olive oil
2 tablespoons lemon juice
1 clove garlic, crushed

PREPARATION TIME 10 MINUTES
COOKING TIME 1 HOUR 25 MINUTES SERVES 4

spanish chicken casserole

1 tablespoon olive oil
4 drumsticks (600g)
4 thigh cutlets (800g)
1 large brown onion (200g), chopped finely
4 medium potatoes (800g), quartered
½ cup (80g) toasted pine nuts
½ cup (80g) toasted blanched almonds
3 cups (750ml) chicken stock
1 cup (250ml) dry white wine
⅓ cup (80ml) lemon juice
4 cloves garlic, crushed
2 tablespoons fresh thyme leaves
½ cup coarsely chopped fresh flat-leaf parsley
500g baby green beans, trimmed

1 Preheat oven to moderate (180°C/160°C fan-forced).
2 Heat oil in large flameproof casserole dish; cook chicken, in batches, until browned.
3 Cook onion in same dish, stirring, until soft. Return chicken to dish with potato, nuts, stock, wine, juice, garlic, thyme and half of the parsley; bring to a boil. Cover; cook in oven about 1 hour or until chicken is cooked through.
4 Meanwhile, boil, steam or microwave beans until tender; drain.
5 Serve chicken with beans; sprinkle with remaining parsley.
per serving 61.4g total fat (12.4g saturated fat); 4050kJ (969 cal); 35g carbohydrate; 57g protein; 10.4g fibre

When using wine in cooking, as a general rule of thumb you should never cook with a wine you wouldn't drink; the wine you use doesn't have to be expensive, but it does have to be drinkable. If you don't want to use white wine, you could substitute water, ginger ale or white grape juice.

chorizo-stuffed roast chicken

PREPARATION TIME 25 MINUTES
COOKING TIME 1 HOUR 35 MINUTES **SERVES** 4

1   Melt half of the butter in medium frying pan; cook onion and chorizo, stirring, until onion softens. Cool 10 minutes; combine chorizo mixture in medium bowl with breadcrumbs, ricotta, egg, parsley and nuts.

2   Preheat oven to moderately hot (200°C/180°C fan-forced).

3   Wash chicken under cold water; pat dry inside and out with absorbent paper. Tuck wing tips under chicken. Trim skin around neck; secure neck flap to underside of chicken with skewers.

4   Fill cavity with chorizo mixture, fold over skin to enclose stuffing; secure with toothpicks. Tie legs together with string. Place chicken and lemon in medium baking dish. Rub chicken all over with remaining butter; roast, uncovered, about 1½ hours or until chicken is cooked through, basting occasionally with juices.

5   Meanwhile, place ingredients for spinach and red onion salad in large bowl; toss gently to combine.

6   Serve chicken with stuffing, lemon and salad.

per serving 68.4g total fat (21.4g saturated fat); 4042kJ (967 cal); 24.4g carbohydrate; 60.3g protein; 5.8g fibre

20g butter

1 medium brown onion (150g), chopped finely

1 chorizo sausage (170g), diced into 1cm pieces

1½ cups (110g) stale breadcrumbs

½ cup (100g) ricotta

1 egg

¼ cup finely chopped fresh flat-leaf parsley

¼ cup (35g) toasted slivered almonds

1.6kg chicken

2 medium lemons (280g), cut into wedges

SPINACH AND RED ONION SALAD

150g baby spinach leaves

1 small red onion (100g), sliced thinly

1 tablespoon red wine vinegar

2 tablespoons olive oil

honey-glazed turkey with orange-pecan stuffing and kumara mash

PREPARATION TIME 30 MINUTES
COOKING TIME 3 HOURS
(PLUS STANDING TIME) SERVES 8

4.5kg turkey
2 medium oranges (480g), unpeeled,
  chopped coarsely
1 cup (250ml) water
2 cups (500ml) chicken stock
½ cup (125ml) bourbon
50g butter, melted
2 tablespoons orange juice
½ cup (175g) honey
2 tablespoons plain flour

ORANGE-PECAN STUFFING
20g butter
1 large brown onion (200g), chopped finely
4 cups (280g) stale breadcrumbs
1 cup (120g) coarsely chopped toasted pecans
1 tablespoon finely grated orange rind
2 tablespoons orange juice
½ cup (125ml) water
40g butter, melted
2 eggs, beaten lightly

KUMARA MASH
3 medium kumara (750g), chopped coarsely
4 medium potatoes (800g), chopped coarsely
⅓ cup (80ml) chicken stock
60g butter, melted

1 Preheat oven to moderate (180°C/160°C fan-forced).
2 Discard neck from turkey. Rinse turkey under cold water; pat dry inside and out with absorbent paper. Tuck wings under turkey; fill large cavity with orange, tie legs together with kitchen string.
3 Place the water, stock and bourbon into large flameproof baking dish; place turkey on oiled wire rack over dish. Brush turkey all over with butter; cover dish tightly with two layers of oiled foil. Roast 2 hours 10 minutes. Uncover turkey; brush with half of the combined orange juice and honey. Roast, uncovered, about 50 minutes or until browned all over and cooked through, brushing frequently with remaining honey mixture. Remove turkey from dish; cover, stand 20 minutes.
4 Meanwhile, make orange-pecan stuffing and kumara mash.
5 Strain turkey juices from dish into large jug. Skim 2 tablespoons of the oil from juices; return oil to dish. Add flour to dish; cook, stirring, until mixture bubbles and browns. Add juices; cook, stirring, until gravy boils and thickens. Strain gravy into same jug.
6 Serve turkey with stuffing, mash and steamed green beans, if desired.
ORANGE-PECAN STUFFING Melt butter in medium frying pan; cook onion, stirring, until soft. Combine onion in medium bowl with breadcrumbs, nuts, rind, juice, water, melted butter and egg. Roll 2 tablespoons of the mixture into balls; place on oiled tray. Bake, uncovered, in oven about 20 minutes or until browned lightly.
KUMARA MASH Boil, steam or microwave kumara and potato, together, until tender; drain. Meanwhile, heat stock in small saucepan until hot. Mash potato and kumara in large bowl until smooth. Stir in hot stock and butter.
per serving 66g total fat (24.2g saturated fat); 5580kJ (1335 cal); 74.9g carbohydrate; 99.6g protein; 7.3g fibre

duck breasts with five-spice and honey peaches

PREPARATION TIME 10 MINUTES
COOKING TIME 20 MINUTES SERVES 4

1   Cook honey, five-spice and peaches in large heated frying pan, stirring, about 5 minutes or until peaches are browned lightly. Remove from pan; cover to keep warm.

2   Score duck skins; cook duck, skin-side down, in same pan, over medium heat, about 10 minutes or until browned and crisp. Turn duck; cook about 5 minutes or until cooked as desired. Remove from pan; cover to keep warm.

3   Combine vinegar, oil, mustard and shallot in large bowl. Add snow peas and spinach; toss gently to combine.

4   Slice duck thinly; serve with peaches and salad.

per serving 17.6g total fat (3.7g saturated fat); 1643kJ (393 cal); 28.2g carbohydrate; 29.4g protein; 3.1g fibre

¼ cup (90g) honey
1 teaspoon five-spice powder
4 medium peaches (600g), quartered
4 duck breast fillets (600g)
1 tablespoon red wine vinegar
2 tablespoons olive oil
1 teaspoon dijon mustard
1 shallot (25g), chopped finely
100g snow peas, trimmed, halved
100g baby spinach leaves

Although ingredients in five-spice powder vary from country to country, it is usually a fragrant ground mixture of cinnamon, clove, star anise, sichuan pepper and fennel seeds.

moroccan chicken with couscous stuffing and green olive salsa

PREPARATION TIME 30 MINUTES
COOKING TIME 2 HOURS 20 MINUTES
(PLUS STANDING TIME) SERVES 4

1   Make couscous stuffing.

2   Preheat oven to moderately hot (200°C/180°C fan-forced).

3   Wash chicken under cold water; pat dry inside and out with absorbent paper. Fill large cavity loosely with couscous stuffing; tie legs together with kitchen string.

4   Half fill a large baking dish with water; place chicken on oiled wire rack over dish. Brush chicken all over with butter; roast, uncovered, 15 minutes. Reduce heat to moderate (180°C/160°C fan-forced); roast, uncovered, about 1½ hours or until cooked through. Remove chicken from rack; cover, stand 20 minutes.

5   Meanwhile, place tomatoes on oven tray; drizzle with oil. Roast, uncovered, about 20 minutes or until softened and browned lightly.

6   Combine ingredients for green olive salsa in small bowl.

7   Serve chicken with tomatoes and salsa.

COUSCOUS STUFFING Heat oil in small frying pan; cook onion, stirring, until onion is soft. Combine stock, extra oil, rind and juice in medium saucepan; bring to a boil. Remove from heat. Add couscous, cover; stand about 5 minutes or until stock is absorbed, fluffing with fork occasionally. Stir in onion, nuts, dates, spices and egg.

per serving 88.7g total fat (19.6g saturated fat); 5756kJ (1377 cal); 77.6g carbohydrate; 65.3g protein; 8.2g fibre

1.6kg chicken
20g butter, melted
20 baby vine-ripened truss tomatoes (400g)
1 tablespoon olive oil

COUSCOUS STUFFING

1 teaspoon olive oil
1 medium brown onion (150g),
   chopped finely
1½ cups (375ml) chicken stock
¼ cup (60ml) olive oil
1 tablespoon finely grated lemon rind
¼ cup (60ml) lemon juice
1 cup (200g) couscous
½ cup (70g) toasted slivered almonds
1 cup (140g) seeded dried dates,
   chopped finely
1 teaspoon ground cinnamon
1 teaspoon smoked paprika
1 egg, beaten lightly

GREEN OLIVE SALSA

1½ cups (180g) seeded green olives,
   chopped coarsely
⅓ cup (80ml) olive oil
1 tablespoon cider vinegar
1 shallot (25g), chopped finely
1 fresh long red chilli, chopped finely
¼ cup coarsely chopped fresh flat-leaf parsley
¼ cup coarsely chopped fresh mint

duck confit with pan-fried kipflers and pear and watercress salad

PREPARATION TIME 1 HOUR
COOKING TIME 3 HOURS SERVES 6

2 x 2kg ducks
1 tablespoon coarse cooking salt
2 cloves garlic, sliced thinly
1 dried bay leaf, crumbled
2 sprigs fresh thyme
2 teaspoons black peppercorns
2 cups (500ml) olive oil, approximately
750g kipfler potatoes, halved lengthways

PEAR AND WATERCRESS SALAD
1 tablespoon wholegrain mustard
1 tablespoon white wine vinegar
1 teaspoon white sugar
¼ cup (60ml) olive oil
350g watercress, trimmed
1 large pear (330g), sliced thinly

1   Using sharp knife, cut marylands and breasts off ducks. Remove as much fat as possible from carcasses; reserve. Discard wings and carcasses.
2   Combine duck pieces, salt, garlic, bay leaf, thyme and peppercorns in medium bowl; cover, refrigerate until required.
3   Meanwhile, place reserved fat in large saucepan; cook, uncovered, over low heat, about 1 hour or until fat has melted. Strain mixture through fine sieve into large bowl; discard solids (you will have approximately 2 cups of duck fat).
4   Preheat oven to slow (150°C/120°C fan-forced).
5   Rinse duck pieces under cold water; pat dry with absorbent paper. Place duck pieces, in single layer, in large baking dish. Reserve 2 tablespoons of the fat; pour remaining fat over duck. Top up with olive oil, making sure duck is completely submerged. Cook, uncovered, in oven 2 hours.
6   Boil, steam or microwave potato until tender; drain. Heat reserved fat in large frying pan; cook potato, in batches, until browned. Cover to keep warm.
7   Meanwhile, make pear and watercress salad.
8   Place duck in same large frying pan; cook, skin-side down, until skin is crisp.
9   Serve duck with potato and salad.
PEAR AND WATERCRESS SALAD Place mustard, vinegar, sugar and oil in screw-top jar; shake well. Place watercress, pear and dressing in large bowl; toss gently to combine.
per serving 184.2g total fat (41.6g saturated fat); 8628kJ (2064 cal); 24.5g carbohydrate; 79.9g protein; 5.5g fibre

Duck carcasses and wings can be used to make stock. Cooked duck can be stored up to 1 month, completely covered in fat, in tightly sealed glass container, in the refrigerator. To reheat duck, remove from fat, wrap in foil and place in very slow oven (120°C/100°C fan-forced) for about 30 minutes.

jambalaya

PREPARATION TIME 10 MINUTES
COOKING TIME 1 HOUR   SERVES 4

1   Cook chorizo in large saucepan, stirring, until browned all over; remove from pan.

2   Cook chicken, in batches, in same pan, until browned all over.

3   Cook onion in same pan, stirring, until onion softens. Add rice, cayenne, thyme, bay leaves, garlic, celery, stock, undrained tomatoes, chorizo and chicken; bring to a boil. Reduce heat; simmer, uncovered, about 15 minutes or until rice is tender and chicken is cooked through.

4   Add peas; cook, uncovered, about 5 minutes or until peas are tender.

per serving 44.9g total fat (14.9g saturated fat); 3942kJ (943 cal); 72.1g carbohydrate; 59.6g protein; 6.6g fibre

1 chorizo sausage (170g), sliced thickly
4 drumsticks (600g)
4 thigh cutlets (800g)
2 medium brown onions (300g), chopped finely
1½ cups (300g) white long-grain rice
¼ teaspoon cayenne pepper
2 teaspoons fresh thyme leaves
2 dried bay leaves
4 cloves garlic, crushed
3 trimmed celery stalks (300g), sliced thickly
3 cups (750ml) chicken stock
400g can crushed tomatoes
1 cup (120g) frozen peas

A creole version of paella, jambalya is believed to have got its name when a cook in New Orleans named Jean tossed together ("balayez", in the Louisiana dialect) various leftovers that resulted in such a delicious dish that it was celebrated with a recipe called "Jean balayez".

The only consistent ingredients among all of the jambalaya recipes are rice, tomatoes, chilli, sausage and onions. Other ingredients can include ham, game birds, chicken, duck, andouille (a smoked, highly-seasoned pork sausage), oysters and prawns.

PREPARATION TIME 15 MINUTES
(PLUS REFRIGERATION TIME)
COOKING TIME 40 MINUTES SERVES 4

southern fried chicken with buttermilk mash and gravy

*Cajun seasoning can be found in the
spice section of your local supermarket.*

20 drumettes (1.4kg)
1 cup (250ml) buttermilk
1 cup (150g) plain flour
¼ cup cajun seasoning
½ cup (125ml) vegetable oil
40g butter
5 medium potatoes (1kg), chopped coarsely
¾ cup (180ml) buttermilk, warmed, extra
40g butter, extra
250g green beans, trimmed,
  cut into 4cm lengths
2 cups (500ml) chicken stock

1   Combine drumettes and buttermilk in large bowl. Cover; refrigerate 3 hours or overnight. Drain; discard buttermilk.
2   Combine flour and seasoning in large bowl; add chicken pieces, toss to coat in mixture. Cover; refrigerate about 30 minutes or until flour forms a paste.
3   Preheat oven to very hot (240°C/220°C fan-forced).
4   Heat oil and butter in large deep frying pan; shake excess paste from drumettes back into bowl. Cook drumettes, in batches, over medium heat until browned and crisp.
5   Place drumettes on wire rack over large baking dish; cook, covered, in oven 15 minutes. Uncover; cook about 10 minutes or until drumettes are cooked through and crisp.
6   Meanwhile, boil, steam or microwave potato until tender; drain. Mash potato in large bowl with extra buttermilk and extra butter until smooth. Cover to keep warm.
7   Boil, steam or microwave beans until tender; drain.
8   To make gravy, add excess paste to pan; cook, stirring, until mixture bubbles. Gradually stir in stock; cook, stirring, until gravy boils and thickens. Strain gravy into large jug.
9   Serve drumettes with mash, beans and gravy.
per serving 69.7g total fat (22.6g saturated fat); 4585kJ (1097 cal); 64.3g carbohydrate; 50.4g protein; 6.6g fibre

panang curry and banana chilli salad

PREPARATION TIME 30 MINUTES
COOKING TIME 30 MINUTES SERVES 4

1   Make panang paste.

2   Meanwhile, combine coconut milk, stock, half of the sauce and half of the sugar in large saucepan; bring to a boil. Add chicken and pumpkin, reduce heat; simmer, uncovered, about 15 minutes or until chicken is cooked through. Strain mixture over large bowl; cover chicken and pumpkin to keep warm, reserve coconut milk mixture.

3   Meanwhile, make banana chilli salad.

4   Bring ½ cup of the coconut milk mixture to a boil in medium frying pan. Boil, uncovered, about 5 minutes or until fat separates from milk. Add panang paste; cook, stirring, 5 minutes. Stir remaining sauce and remaining sugar into mixture; stir until sugar dissolves. Add 1 cup of the remaining coconut milk mixture, reduce heat; simmer, uncovered, until heated through. (Discard any left over coconut milk mixture.)

5   Top chicken and pumpkin with panang sauce; serve with salad, and lime wedges, if desired.

PANANG PASTE Preheat oven to moderate (180°C/160°C fan-forced). Place shallots and nuts on oven tray; roast, uncovered, about 15 minutes or until nuts are browned lightly, cool 10 minutes. Blend or process shallots and nuts with remaining ingredients until mixture forms a coarse paste.

BANANA CHILLI SALAD Cook chillies and shallots on heated oiled grill plate (or grill or barbecue) until tender; slice thickly. Combine sugar, juice and sauce in medium bowl. Add chillies, shallots and coriander; toss gently to combine.

per serving 43.7g total fat (24.8g saturated fat); 2955kJ (707 cal); 25g carbohydrate; 51.9g protein; 6.7g fibre

If you cannot find banana chillies, use capsicums instead.

1⅔ cups (410ml) coconut milk
1½ cups (375ml) chicken stock
2 tablespoons fish sauce
2 tablespoons grated palm sugar
8 thigh fillets (880g), sliced thickly
500g pumpkin, diced into 2cm pieces

PANANG PASTE
2 purple shallots (50g)
⅓ cup (45g) unsalted peanuts
2 fresh long red chillies, chopped coarsely
1 teaspoon finely chopped coriander root
3cm piece fresh galangal (15g), grated
5cm stick (10g) finely chopped
   fresh lemon grass
2 cloves garlic, crushed
1 teaspoon shrimp paste

BANANA CHILLI SALAD
2 green banana chillies (250g)
2 red banana chillies (250g)
4 purple shallots (100g)
2 teaspoons grated palm sugar
1 tablespoon lime juice
2 teaspoons fish sauce
½ cup loosely packed fresh coriander leaves

PREPARATION TIME 15 MINUTES
(PLUS REFRIGERATION TIME)
COOKING TIME 45 MINUTES SERVES 4

portuguese-style chicken

3 fresh small red thai chillies, chopped finely
2 teaspoons dried chilli flakes
3 cloves garlic, crushed
¼ cup (60ml) cider vinegar
2 teaspoons finely grated lemon rind
⅔ cup (160ml) lemon juice
2 teaspoons smoked paprika
½ cup finely chopped fresh flat-leaf parsley
2 teaspoons coarse cooking salt
¼ teaspoon cracked black pepper
2 tablespoons olive oil
4 marylands (1.4kg)
80g mesclun

1   Combine chillies, garlic, vinegar, rind, juice, paprika, parsley, salt, pepper and oil in large bowl, add chicken; turn to coat in marinade. Cover; refrigerate overnight.

2   Cook chicken, covered, on heated oiled grill plate (or grill or barbecue), over medium heat, about 45 minutes or until cooked through.

3   Serve chicken with mesclun, and lemon wedges, if desired.
per serving 41.8g total fat (11.7g saturated fat); 2337kJ (559 cal); 1.5g carbohydrate; 43g protein; 1.1g fibre

Sometimes sold as spring salad mix, mesclun is a commercial assortment of young green leaves, and will usually include some or all of the following: rocket, mizuna, baby spinach, curly endive, oak leaf, radicchio and mignonette.

italian roasted quail
with braised vegetables

PREPARATION TIME 15 MINUTES
COOKING TIME 45 MINUTES SERVES 4

1 Preheat oven to moderately hot (200°C/180°C fan-forced).

2 Discard necks from quails. Wash quails under cold water; pat dry inside and out with absorbent paper. Tuck legs along body; wrap tightly with prosciutto to hold legs in place.

3 Heat butter in large flameproof baking dish; cook quails, in batches, until browned all over.

4 Place wine in same dish; bring to a boil. Reduce heat; simmer, uncovered, until wine has reduced to 1 tablespoon. Add fennel, garlic, capsicum, zucchini and stock; return to a boil. Place quails on top of vegetables; roast, uncovered, in oven 20 minutes. Add lemon to dish; roast, uncovered, about 10 minutes or until quails are cooked through.

5 Remove quails and garlic from dish. When cool enough to handle, squeeze garlic from skins into dish; stir in cream and oregano.

6 Serve quails on vegetables.

per serving 30.8g total fat (12.4g saturated fat); 2052kJ (491 cal); 6.9g carbohydrate; 39.1g protein; 4.2g fibre

8 quails (1.3kg)
8 slices prosciutto (120g)
20g butter
½ cup (125ml) dry white wine
2 baby fennel bulbs (260g),
   trimmed, sliced thinly
4 cloves garlic, unpeeled
1 large red capsicum (350g), sliced thinly
2 medium zucchini (240g), halved
   lengthways, sliced thickly
½ cup (125ml) chicken stock
1 medium lemon (140g),
   cut into eight wedges
¼ cup (60ml) cream
1 tablespoon fresh oregano leaves

pot roast with
mustard cream sauce

PREPARATION TIME 25 MINUTES
COOKING TIME 1 HOUR 50 MINUTES SERVES 4

1.6kg chicken
1 tablespoon olive oil
12 shallots (300g), halved
20 baby carrots (400g), trimmed
3 small parsnips (360g), chopped coarsely
1 cup (250ml) dry white wine
2 cups (500ml) chicken stock
2 dried bay leaves
200g swiss brown mushrooms
2 tablespoons cream
2 tablespoons wholegrain mustard

1   Preheat oven to moderately hot (200°C/180°C fan-forced).
2   Wash chicken under cold water; pat dry inside and out with absorbent paper.
3   Heat oil in large flameproof casserole dish; cook chicken until browned all over. Remove chicken. Cook shallots, carrots and parsnips in same dish, stirring, about 5 minutes or until vegetables are browned lightly.
4   Return chicken to dish with wine, stock and bay leaves; bring to a boil. Cook, covered, in oven 30 minutes. Uncover; cook about 30 minutes or until chicken is cooked through. Add mushrooms; cook, uncovered, about 10 minutes or until mushrooms are tender.
5   Remove chicken and vegetables from dish; cover to keep warm. Add cream and mustard to dish; bring to a boil. Boil, uncovered, about 5 minutes or until sauce thickens slightly.
6   Serve chicken with vegetables and mustard cream sauce.
per serving 42.2g total fat (13.8g saturated fat); 2859kJ (684 cal); 16.9g carbohydrate; 46.7g protein; 6.6g fibre

Swiss brown mushrooms, also known as roman or cremini, are light-to dark-brown in colour with a full bodied flavour. Store on a tray in a single layer, covered with damp, absorbent paper and keep where cool air can circulate around them.

quince and chicken tagine

PREPARATION TIME 25 MINUTES
COOKING TIME 1 HOUR 50 MINUTES SERVES 4

1 Place quinces, butter, honey, the water and orange flower water in medium saucepan; bring to a boil. Reduce heat; simmer, covered, 1 hour, stirring occasionally. Uncover, cook, stirring occasionally, about 45 minutes or until quinces are red in colour.

2 Meanwhile, heat oil in large frying pan; cook chicken, in batches, until browned. Cook onion, garlic and spices in same pan, stirring, until onion softens. Add stock and chicken; bring to a boil. Reduce heat; simmer, covered, 20 minutes. Uncover; simmer, about 20 minutes or until chicken is cooked though. Add zucchini; cook, uncovered, about 10 minutes or until zucchini is tender. Stir in quinces and ½ cup of the quince syrup.

3 Meanwhile, make coriander couscous.

4 Divide tagine and couscous among serving plates; sprinkle tagine with coriander.

CORIANDER COUSCOUS Combine couscous with the water in large heatproof bowl; cover, stand about 5 minutes or until water is absorbed, fluffing with fork occasionally. Stir in spinach, coriander and onion.

per serving 32.6g total fat (12.3g saturated fat); 3913kJ (936 cal); 99g carbohydrate; 56.7g protein; 12.5g fibre

2 medium quinces (700g), peeled, cored, cut into wedges
40g butter
⅓ cup (115g) honey
3 cups (750ml) water
2 teaspoons orange flower water
2 teaspoons olive oil
4 drumsticks (600g)
4 thigh cutlets (800g), skin removed
1 large brown onion (200g), chopped coarsely
3 cloves garlic, crushed
1 teaspoon ground cumin
1 teaspoon ground ginger
pinch saffron threads
2 cups (500ml) chicken stock
2 large zucchini (300g), chopped coarsely
¼ cup coarsely chopped fresh coriander

CORIANDER COUSCOUS
1½ cups (300g) couscous
1½ cups (375ml) boiling water
50g baby spinach leaves, chopped finely
2 tablespoons finely chopped fresh coriander
2 green onions, sliced thinly

PREPARATION TIME 20 MINUTES
COOKING TIME 1 HOUR 10 MINUTES SERVES 4

fricassee

40g butter
8 shallots (200g), peeled
20 baby carrots (400g), halved
1kg thigh fillets, cut into thirds
2 tablespoons plain flour
½ cup (125ml) dry white wine
1½ cups (375g) chicken stock
2 tablespoons dijon mustard
2 large kumara (1kg), chopped coarsely
20g butter, extra
½ cup (125ml) cream
2 egg yolks
¼ cup (60ml) cream, extra
1 tablespoon lemon juice
2 tablespoons coarsely chopped fresh tarragon

1 Heat butter in large heavy-based saucepan; cook shallots and carrots, over low heat, stirring occasionally, about 5 minutes or until browned lightly, remove from pan. Cook chicken, in batches, in same pan, over low heat, until browned lightly.

2 Add flour; cook, stirring, until mixture bubbles and thickens. Gradually stir in combined wine, stock and mustard. Return chicken to pan with shallots and carrots; bring to a boil. Reduce heat; simmer, covered, about 45 minutes or until chicken is cooked through.

3 Meanwhile, boil, steam or microwave kumara until tender; drain. Mash kumara with extra butter and cream in large bowl until smooth. Cover to keep warm.

4 Combine egg yolks, extra cream, juice and tarragon in medium jug. Remove fricassee from heat. Gradually add cream mixture, stirring constantly.

5 Serve fricassee with mash.

per serving 54.1g total fat (27.9g saturated fat); 3825kJ (915 cal); 43.5g carbohydrate; 56.4g protein; 7.6g fibre

When making kumara mash, ensure that you do not overcook the kumara, otherwise the mash will become wet and runny. For a twist, flavour your kumara mash with crushed, roasted garlic, orange juice, chives, nutmeg or any herbs, finely chopped, of your choice.

oyako donburi

PREPARATION TIME 30 MINUTES
(PLUS STANDING TIME)
COOKING TIME 45 MINUTES SERVES 4

1   Place mushrooms in small heatproof bowl; cover with boiling water, stand 20 minutes, drain. Discard stems; chop caps coarsely. Combine dashi with the boiling water in small jug.

2   Meanwhile, heat oil in large frying pan; cook brown onion and ginger, stirring, over medium heat, about 10 minutes or until onion is slightly caramelised. Add half of the dashi mixture, reduce heat; simmer, about 5 minutes or until liquid evaporates. Transfer to medium bowl.

3   Bring rice and the cold water to a boil in large saucepan, uncovered, stirring occasionally. Reduce heat to as low as possible; cover with a tight-fitting lid, cook rice 12 minutes. (Do not remove lid or stir rice during cooking time.) Remove from heat; stand, covered, 10 minutes.

4   Meanwhile, combine sauce, mirin, sugar and remaining dashi mixture to same frying pan; bring to a boil. Add chicken and mushrooms; cook, covered, about 5 minutes or until chicken is cooked through.

5   Combine egg with brown onion mixture in medium bowl; add onion mixture to chicken mixture. Cook, covered, over low heat, about 5 minutes or until egg just sets.

6   Divide rice among bowls; top with chicken mixture and green onion.

per serving 15.8g total fat (4.1g saturated fat); 2567kJ (614 cal); 67.6g carbohydrate; 46.2g protein; 2.7g fibre

4 dried shiitake mushrooms
2 teaspoons dashi powder
1 cup (250ml) boiling water
1 tablespoon peanut oil
3 large brown onions (600g), sliced thinly
1cm piece fresh ginger (5g), grated
1½ cups (300g) koshihikari rice
3 cups (750ml) cold water
¼ cup (60ml) japanese soy sauce
¼ cup (60ml) mirin
1 teaspoon white sugar
500g breast fillets, sliced thinly
6 eggs, beaten lightly
2 green onions, sliced thinly

Donburi refers both to a particular shaped bowl as well as the rice-based main course that is served in it. Oyako translates to "parent and child" in Japanese, which, in this case, refers to the chicken and the egg. You can substitute a white medium-grain rice if koshihikari is unavailable.

PREPARATION TIME 30 MINUTES
(PLUS REFRIGERATION TIME)
COOKING TIME 1 HOUR SERVES 4

peking duck

You can buy pancakes at your local Asian grocery store. Plain hoisin sauce can be substituted for the peanut and hoisin sauce, if desired.

2kg duck
⅓ cup (80ml) water
1 tablespoon treacle
1 teaspoon rice vinegar
1 tablespoon dry sherry
1 teaspoon five-spice powder
4cm piece fresh ginger (20g), sliced thickly
2 star anise
1 lebanese cucumber (130g)
5 green onions

PANCAKES
2 cups (300g) plain flour
1 cup (250ml) boiling water
2 teaspoons peanut oil

PEANUT AND HOISIN SAUCE
1 tablespoon peanut butter
2 tablespoons hoisin sauce
1 tablespoon peanut oil
1 tablespoon sake

1 Wash duck under cold water; pat dry inside and out with absorbent paper. Tie string around neck of duck. Lower duck into large saucepan of boiling water for 30 seconds; remove from pan. Drain well; pat dry with absorbent paper. Tie string to refrigerator shelf and suspend duck, uncovered, over drip tray overnight.
2 Preheat oven to very hot (240°C/220°C fan-forced).
3 Tuck wings under duck. Place duck, breast-side up, on wire rack in large baking dish; brush entire duck with combined water, treacle, vinegar, sherry and five-spice. Place ginger and star anise inside cavity of duck. Roast, uncovered, 10 minutes; turn duck breast-side down. Brush with marinade; roast, uncovered, 10 minutes. Turn duck breast-side up; brush with marinade.
4 Reduce oven temperature to moderately hot (200°C/180°C fan-forced); roast, uncovered, brushing occasionally with remaining marinade, about 30 minutes or until duck is cooked as desired.
5 Increase oven temperature to very hot (240°C/220°C fan-forced); roast, uncovered, about 10 minutes or until skin is crisp and browned.
6 Meanwhile, make pancakes.
7 Combine ingredients for peanut and hoisin sauce in small bowl.
8 Place duck on chopping board; remove skin. Slice skin and duck meat thickly.
9 Using teaspoon, remove seeds from cucumber. Cut cucumber and onions into 5cm strips. Serve warm pancakes with duck meat, crisp skin, cucumber, onion and sauce.
PANCAKES Sift flour into large bowl; add the water, stir quickly using wooden spoon until ingredients cling together. Knead dough on floured surface about 10 minutes or until smooth. Divide dough into 20 pieces; roll pieces into balls, flatten slightly. Brush tops of dough with oil. Place one piece of dough on top of another, oiled surfaces together; roll out into an 18cm pancake. Repeat with remaining balls. Cook pancakes, one at a time, in small lightly oiled frying pan, over medium heat, about 30 seconds or until browned lightly. Turn pancake; brown other side. Pull pancakes apart with fingers to make two thin pancakes. Wrap pancakes in foil after each is cooked to prevent drying out.
per serving 27.2g total fat (6.6g saturated fat); 3219kJ (770 cal); 64.6g carbohydrate; 61.2g protein; 5.5g fibre

harissa spatchcock with rocket and cucumber salad

PREPARATION TIME 25 MINUTES
COOKING TIME 20 MINUTES SERVES 4

1   Rinse spatchcocks under cold water; pat dry inside and out with absorbent paper. Using kitchen scissors, cut along each side of each spatchcock's backbone; discard backbone. Place spatchcocks, skin-side up, on board; using heel of hand, press down on breastbone to flatten spatchcock.

2   Combine paste, rind and 1 tablespoon of the oil in large bowl, add spatchcock; rub mixture all over spatchcock.

3   Cook spatchcock on heated oiled grill plate (or grill or barbecue), uncovered, 10 minutes. Cover, cook, over low heat, about 10 minutes or until spatchcocks are cooked through.

4   Meanwhile, dry-fry spices in small frying pan, stirring, until fragrant. Cool 10 minutes. Combine spices with yogurt and garlic in small bowl.

5   Using vegetable peeler, slice cucumber lengthways into ribbons. Combine cucumber in large bowl with rocket, juice and remaining oil.

6   Serve spatchcock with yogurt and salad.

per serving 55.2g total fat (15.4g saturated fat); 3043kJ (728 cal); 4.9g carbohydrate; 52.8g protein; 1.5g fibre

4 x 500g spatchcocks
1 tablespoon harissa paste
1 teaspoon finely grated lemon rind
¼ cup (60ml) olive oil
2 teaspoons cumin seeds
1 teaspoon ground coriander
200g yogurt
1 clove garlic, crushed
2 lebanese cucumbers (260g)
150g baby rocket leaves
2 tablespoons lemon juice

A Moroccan sauce or paste made from dried chillies, garlic oil and caraway seeds, harissa can be used as a rub for meats, a sauce or dressing ingredient, or a condiment eaten on its own. It is available in supermarkets and Middle Eastern food shops.

PREPARATION TIME 25 MINUTES
COOKING TIME 1 HOUR 20 MINUTES
(PLUS STANDING TIME) SERVES 4

barbecued lemon thyme chicken

6 cloves garlic, sliced thickly
3 shallots (75g), chopped finely
½ cup (125ml) chicken stock
20g butter, softened
1 tablespoon finely chopped fresh lemon thyme
1.6kg chicken
600g kipfler potatoes, halved lengthways
340g asparagus, trimmed
1 medium lemon (140g), quartered
1 tablespoon olive oil

1   Place garlic, shallot and stock in small saucepan; bring to a boil. Reduce heat; simmer, uncovered, about 20 minutes or until garlic is soft and liquid is almost evaporated. Cool 5 minutes; stir in butter and thyme.

2   Wash chicken under cold water; pat dry inside and out with absorbent paper. Using kitchen scissors, cut along each side of backbone; discard backbone. Place chicken, skin-side up, on board. Using heel of hand, press down on breastbone to flatten chicken. Make a pocket between chicken and skin; push thyme mixture under skin.

3   Cook chicken, skin-side down, on heated oiled grill plate (or grill or barbecue), covered, over medium heat, 15 minutes. Turn chicken; cook, covered, about 35 minutes or until cooked through. Cover; stand 15 minutes.

4   Meanwhile, boil, steam or microwave potato until just tender; drain. Cook potato, asparagus and lemon on same grill plate (or grill or barbecue) brushing with the oil, until browned.

5   Serve chicken with potato, asparagus and lemon.

per serving 41.4g total fat (13.5g saturated fat); 2776kJ (664 cal); 22.8g carbohydrate; 46.7g protein; 5.4g fibre

A member of the lily family, asparagus is a delicious vegetable with a delicate, nutty flavour that can be eaten raw or cooked. The woody stems of the spears should be removed before cooking or eating, and any especially hard, tough stems should be peeled.

greek-style drumsticks with olives and artichokes

PREPARATION TIME 15 MINUTES
COOKING TIME 1 HOUR SERVES 4

1 Heat half of the oil in large heavy-based saucepan; cook drumsticks, in batches, until browned all over.

2 Heat remaining oil in same pan; cook onion and garlic, stirring, until onion softens. Add rind, stock, wine and artichokes; bring to a boil. Return drumsticks to pan, reduce heat; simmer, covered, 20 minutes. Uncover; simmer, about 10 minutes or until drumsticks are cooked through.

3 Meanwhile, cook risoni in large saucepan of boiling water, uncovered, until just tender; drain.

4 Remove chicken from pan; stir oregano, olives, extra juice and extra rind into sauce.

5 Serve chicken with sauce on risoni.

per serving 44.7g total fat (11.7g saturated fat); 4631kJ (1108 cal); 98.7g carbohydrate; 67.8g protein; 5.7g fibre

2 tablespoons olive oil
12 drumsticks (1.8kg)
1 medium white onion (150g), chopped finely
3 cloves garlic, crushed
1 tablespoon finely grated lemon rind
1½ cups (375ml) chicken stock
½ cup (125ml) dry white wine
340g jar marinated artichokes,
   drained, quartered
500g risoni
2 tablespoons finely chopped fresh oregano
1 cup (150g) seeded kalamata olives
1 tablespoon finely grated lemon rind, extra
¼ cup (60ml) lemon juice

Risoni, also known as risi, is a very small rice-shaped pasta similar to orzo. It is great added to soups, baked in a casserole or as a side dish when served with a main course.

ABOUT POULTRY

Advice on storing and handling, identifying the various cuts and hints for the perfect roast.

keep it clean

Keep poultry separate from other foods in the refrigerator. Poultry should also remain refrigerated until you're ready to start cooking. Reserve one plastic cutting board exclusively for raw poultry (and meat) and scrub it well with hot water and soap after every use. Wash everything else you've used, including your hands, after dealing with raw poultry.

commonly used cuts

Breast fillet all skin and bones removed. When a recipe calls for breast fillet, this is a single breast fillet. **Tenderloin** the thin, tender strip of meat lying just under the breast. **Thigh cutlet** skin-on, with one bone in the centre; sometimes sold as a chicken chop. **Thigh fillet** skin and bones removed. **Wing** skin-on with bones intact; has very little meat. **Drumette** wing trimmed to resemble drumstick; tip of the bone chopped off. **Drumstick** leg having skin and bones intact. **Maryland** connected leg and thigh piece; bones and skin intact. **Mince** ground thigh or breast meat. **Strips** boneless, skinless, stir-fry-sized pieces of either thigh or breast meat. **Spatchcock** a small chicken (poussin), no more than 6 weeks old, weighing a maximum 500g. **Barbecued chicken** sold already cooked; available from supermarkets, delicatessens and chicken-speciality stores.

trussing & roasting

Securing the neck, legs and wings of a bird with kitchen string so that it holds its shape during cooking is called trussing. Tie the string first around the tail or "parson's nose", then around the legs, bringing it between the legs and body toward the wings. Wrap the string around the wings then turn bird over and knot it firmly between the wings. Tuck the neck flap under, securing it to the bird with a toothpick or skewer.

To roast, place the bird on a metal rack set inside a shallow baking dish, or simply sit it directly on the bottom of the dish. Cook, uncovered, according to the recipe's directions. Don't baste too often as every time you open the oven door the temperature drops and could lead to either an undercooked bird or a long cooking time. Frequent basting can also prevent the skin from crisping and browning. Prevent overbrowning by covering with foil. Rest for a few minutes out of the oven before cutting.

storing & thawing

It's important, given our warm climate, that poultry is stored appropriately, handled carefully and cooked correctly. The longer food is at room temperature, the greater the chance of food poisoning becomes. Take an insulated bag (or even a freezer brick) when you go shopping, and purchase all poultry products last. As soon as you get home, re-wrap and refrigerate poultry in the coldest part of your refrigerator, or freeze it. Defrost poultry in the refrigerator. Once thawed, never refreeze raw poultry. Raw whole birds or pieces can only safely be kept in the refrigerator for 2 days at most, and chicken mince and sausages for 1 day. Keep filling and bird, covered separately, under refrigeration until you're ready to stuff and cook it. Refrigerate leftover cooked chicken immediately.

GLOSSARY

ALLSPICE also known as pimento or jamaican pepper; tastes like a blend of clove, cinnamon and nutmeg.

ARTICHOKE, GLOBE large flower-bud of a member of the thistle family, having tough petal-like leaves; edible in part when cooked. Artichoke hearts, the tender centre of the globe artichoke, can be harvested fresh from the plant or purchased in brine canned or in glass jars.

BACON RASHERS also known as bacon slices; made from cured and smoked pork side.

BAMBOO SHOOTS the tender shoots of bamboo plants, available in cans; must be drained and rinsed before use.

BEANS
broad also known as fava, windsor and horse beans; are available dried, fresh, canned and frozen. Fresh and frozen, they are best peeled twice (discarding both the outer long green pod and the beige-green tough inner shell).
snake long (about 40cm), thin, round, fresh green beans, also known as yard-long beans because of their length.
sprouts also known as bean shoots; tender new growths of assorted beans and seeds germinated for consumption as sprouts.

BOK CHOY also known as bak choy, pak choy and chinese white cabbage; has a mild mustard taste. *Baby bok choy* is smaller and more tender and often cooked whole.

BREADCRUMBS
packaged fine-textured, crunchy, purchased white breadcrumbs.
stale one- or two-day-old bread made into crumbs by blending or processing.

BROCCOLINI a cross between broccoli and chinese kale, is milder and sweeter than traditional broccoli. Substitute chinese broccoli (gai larn) or common broccoli.

BUTTERMILK originally just the liquid left after cream was separated from milk, today it is commercially made similarly to yogurt.

CAJUN SEASONING a blend of herbs and spices including basil, paprika, tarragon, onion, fennel, thyme and cayenne.

CAPSICUM also known as bell pepper or, simply, pepper. Discard seeds and membranes before use.

CARAWAY SEEDS a member of the parsley family, available in seed or ground form.

CARDAMOM native to India; available in pod, seed or ground form. Has a distinctive aromatic, sweetly rich flavour.

CELERIAC tuberous root with brown skin, white flesh and a celery-like flavour.

CHAR SIU SAUCE a chinese barbecue sauce made from sugar, water, salt, fermented soybean paste, honey, soy sauce, malt syrup and spices. Available from Asian food stores and most supermarkets.

CHEESE
fetta a crumbly goat- or sheep-milk cheese with a sharp, salty taste.
goat made from goat milk, has an earthy, strong taste; available in both soft and firm.
gruyere a swiss cheese having small holes and a nutty, salty flavour.
haloumi a firm, sheep-milk cheese; has a minty, salty, fetta-like flavour. Haloumi can be grilled or fried, briefly, without breaking down.
mozzarella soft cheese originally made from water buffalo milk.

parmesan also known as parmigiano; a hard, grainy cow-milk cheese. The curd is salted in brine for a month before being aged for up to two years.
provolone a mild cheese, similar to mozzarella when young. Golden yellow colour, with a smooth shiny skin.
ricotta a low-fat, fresh unripened cheese made from whey.
romano a hard, straw-coloured sheep-milk cheese; mainly used for grating. Parmesan can be substituted.

CHERVIL also known as cicily; mildly fennel-flavoured herb with curly dark-green leaves.

CHICKEN CUTS
breast skin and bone intact.
breast fillet breast halved, skinned and boned.
drumettes small fleshy part of a chicken wing between the shoulder and elbow.
drumstick leg with skin intact.
maryland leg and thigh still connected in a single piece and bones and skin intact.
mince known as ground meat.
tenderloin thin strip of meat lying just under the breast; good for stir-fry cooking.
thigh skin and bone intact.
thigh cutlet with skin and bone intact; sometimes known as a chicken chop.
thigh fillet has skin and bone removed.

CHICKPEAS also called garbanzos, hummus or channa; an irregularly round, sandy-coloured legume used extensively in Mediterranean and Latin cooking.

CHILLIES available fresh and dried in many different types and sizes; Generally, the smaller the chilli, the hotter it is. Use rubber gloves when seeding and chopping fresh chillies, as they can burn your skin.

banana a sweet-flavoured chilli with a long, tapering shape. If unavailable, substitute with red capsicum.
cayenne a thin-fleshed, long, extremely hot red chilli; usually purchased dried and ground.
red thai small, bright red, medium-hot chilli.

CHILLI JAM a sweet, sourish tangy jam that is sold in jars at supermarkets or Asian food stores. Used in sauces, stir-fries and some soups. After opening, store it in the refrigerator.

CHINESE CABBAGE also known as peking or napa cabbage; elongated in shape, with pale green, crinkly leaves.

CHINESE COOKING WINE made from rice, wheat, sugar and salt, with 13.5% alcohol; available from Asian food stores. Mirin or sherry can be substituted.

CHORIZO a sausage of Spanish origin, made of coarsely ground pork and highly seasoned with garlic and chillies.

CIABATTA in Italian, the word means slipper, which is the traditional shape of this white crispy crusted bread.

CONFIT a preserved food item that is salted and cooked slowly in its own fat. Usually a fatty meat such as duck, goose or pork is used, although any meat, or fruit or vegetable, can be preserved as a confit, using oil or lard.

CORIANDER also known as cilantro or chinese parsley; bright-green-leafed herb with a pungent flavour. Stems and roots can be used. Also sold as seeds, whole or ground.

COUSCOUS a fine, grain-like cereal product, originally from North Africa; made from semolina.

CRANBERRY SAUCE sold in jars in two varieties: whole berry or jellied.

CUCUMBER, LEBANESE also known as the european or burpless cucumber.

CUMIN also known as zeera, available in ground or seed form from supermarkets.

DASHI a seaweed and fish stock often used in Japanese cooking; made from dried bonito (tuna) flakes and kelp (kombu). Available from Asian food stores.

DUCK FAT can be kept in the fridge for up to three months; it is great used for roasting vegetables.

EGG some recipes in this book call for raw or barely cooked eggs; exercise caution if there is a salmonella problem in your area.

EGGPLANT also known as aubergine. Ranges in size from tiny to very large and in colour from pale green to deep purple.

FENNEL also known as anise or finocchio; also the name of dried seeds that have a licorice flavour.

FISH SAUCE also called nam pla or nuoc nam; made from pulverised salted fermented fish, most often anchovies. Has a pungent smell and strong taste, so use sparingly.

FIVE-SPICE POWDER a fragrant mix of ground cloves, cinnamon, star anise, sichuan pepper and fennel seeds.

GAI LARN also known as chinese broccoli or chinese kale; its stems are used more often than its coarse leaves.

GALANGAL also known as ka, a rhizome with a hot ginger-citrusy flavour. Fresh ginger can be substituted for fresh galangal, but the flavour will not be the same.

GARAM MASALA a blend of spices that includes cloves, cardamom, cinnamon, cumin, coriander and fennel.

GINGER
fresh also known as green or root ginger.
ground also known as powdered ginger; cannot be substituted for fresh ginger.

HARISSA PASTE made from dried red chillies, garlic, oil and sometimes caraway seeds.

HOISIN SAUCE a thick, sweet and spicy chinese paste made from salted fermented soy beans, onions and garlic.

KAFFIR LIME LEAVES also known as bai magrood, sold fresh, dried or frozen; looks like two glossy dark green leaves joined end to end, forming a rounded hourglass shape. A strip of fresh lime peel may be substituted for each kaffir lime leaf.

KECAP MANIS also known as ketjap manis; a thick soy sauce with added sugar and spices.

KIPFLER POTATOES small, finger-shaped potato with a nutty flavour and pale yellow skin and flesh.

KITCHEN STRING made of a natural product, such as cotton or hemp, so it neither affects the flavour of the food, nor melts when heated.

KUMARA Polynesian name of orange-fleshed sweet potato often confused with yam.

LAMB'S LETTUCE also known as mâche, corn salad or lamb tongue, the tender narrow dark-green leaves have a mild, almost nutty flavour.

LEMON GRASS a tall, clumping, lemon-smelling and tasting, sharp-edged grass. The white lower part of each stem is chopped and used in cooking.

LEMON MYRTLE similar in appearance to bay leaves; have an aroma redolent of lemon grass, lemon and lime, lemon verbena and kaffir lime.

MAPLE SYRUP a thick syrup distilled from the sap of the maple tree. Maple-flavoured syrup or pancake syrup is not an adequate substitute.

MESCLUN a salad mix of assorted young lettuce and other green leaves, including baby spinach, mizuna, curly endive.

MIRIN is a Japanese champagne-coloured cooking wine expressly for cooking; should not be confused with sake.

MUSHROOMS
flat large, with a rich earthy flavour, ideal for filling and barbecuing. Are sometimes misnamed field mushrooms, which are wild mushrooms.
shiitake when fresh are also known as chinese black, forest or golden oak mushrooms. Are large and meaty with the earthiness and taste of wild mushrooms. When dried, they are known as donko or dried chinese mushrooms; rehydrate before use.
swiss brown also known as cremini or roman mushrooms; light to dark brown in colour with full-bodied flavour. Button or cup mushrooms can be substituted.

MUSTARD
dijon a pale brown, fairly mild french mustard.
seeds, yellow also known as white mustard seeds; less pungent than the black variety. Available from supermarkets or health food shops.
wholegrain also known as seeded mustard; coarse-grain mustard made from black, yellow or brown mustard seeds and a dijon-style mustard.

NOODLES
fried crispy egg noodles already deep-fried.
rice stick also known as sen lek, ho fun or kway teow; especially popular South-East Asian dried rice noodle. Come in different widths (thin, used in soups, and wide, used in stir-fries) but all should be soaked in hot water until soft.
two-minute quick cooking noodles also known as instant noodles with flavour sachet.
udon available both fresh and dried, these Japanese broad white wheat noodles are similar to those in homemade chicken noodle soup.

ORANGE FLOWER WATER concentrated flavouring made from orange blossoms. Available from Middle-Eastern food stores, delicatessens and some supermarkets. Cannot be substituted with citrus flavourings, as the taste is completely different.

OYSTER SAUCE Asian in origin; this sauce is made from oysters and their brine, cooked with salt and soy sauce and thickened with starches.

PANCETTA an Italian-style bacon; cured, but not smoked.

PAPRIKA ground dried red capsicum (bell pepper), available sweet or hot.

PARSLEY, FLAT-LEAF also known as continental or italian parsley.

PITTA also known as lebanese bread. A wheat-flour pocket bread sold in large, flat pieces that separate into two thin rounds. Also available in small thick pieces called pocket pitta.

POLENTA also known as cornmeal; a flour-like cereal made of dried corn (maize) sold ground in several different textures; also the name of the dish made from it.

PROSCIUTTO cured, air-dried (unsmoked), pressed ham; usually sold thinly sliced.

QUAIL small, delicately flavoured, domestically grown game birds weighing from 250g to 300g; also known as partridge.

QUINCE yellow-skinned fruit with hard texture and astringent, tart taste; eaten cooked or as a preserve.

RICE
arborio small, round grain rice well-suited to absorb a large amount of liquid; especially suitable for risottos.
basmati a fragrant long-grained white rice.
jasmine fragrant long-grained rice; white rice can be substituted, but the dish will not taste the same.
koshihikari small, round-grain white rice. If unavailable, substitute white short-grain rice and cook using the absorption method.

ROCKET also known as arugula, rugula and rucola; a peppery-tasting green leaf that can be used similarly to baby spinach leaves. *Baby rocket leaves* are both smaller and less peppery.

SAFFRON stigma of a member of the crocus family, available in strands or ground form; imparts a yellow-orange colour to food once infused. Quality varies greatly; the best is the most expensive spice in the world. Should be stored in the freezer.

SAKE Japan's favourite rice wine. If unavailable, brandy, dry sherry or vermouth can be substituted.

SHALLOTS also called french shallots, golden shallots or eschalots; small, elongated, brown-skinned members of the onion family.

SHRIMP PASTE known also as kapi, trasi and blanchan; a strong-scented, very firm preserved paste made of salted dried shrimp. Used as a pungent flavouring in many South-East Asian soups and sauces.

SICHUAN PEPPERCORNS also known as szechuan or chinese pepper. A mildly hot spice with a distinctive peppery-lemon flavour and aroma.

SNOW PEAS also called mange tout ('eat all'). *Snow pea tendrils*, the growing shoots of the plant, are available from greengrocers and supermarkets.

SOY SAUCE also known as sieu, is made from fermented soy beans.
japanese lighter, less dense and less salty than chinese soy sauce.

SPATCHCOCK a small chicken (poussin), no more than six weeks old, weighing a maximum 500g. Also, a cooking technique where a small chicken is split open, then flattened and grilled.

SPINACH also known as english spinach and, incorrectly, silver beet; also available as baby spinach leaves, which are smaller versions of the adult vegetable. Its tender green leaves are good uncooked in salads or added to soups, stir-fries and stews just before serving.

SPRING ONION vegetable having a small white, walnut-sized bulb, long green leaves and narrow green-leafed tops.

STAR ANISE a dried star-shaped fruit of a tree native to China. The pods, which have an astringent aniseed or licorice flavour, are widely used in the Asian kitchen. Available whole and ground, it is an essential ingredient in five-spice powder.

STOCK cubes, powder or concentrated liquid can be used. As a guide, 1 small stock cube or 1 teaspoon of stock powder or 1 portion stock concentrate mixed with 1 cup (250ml) water will give a fairly strong stock. Also available in ready-to-use bottles, cans or tetra packs.

SUGAR
palm also known as nam tan pip, jaggery, jawa or gula melaka; made from the sap of the sugar palm tree. Light brown to black in colour and usually sold in rock-hard cakes; substitute it with brown sugar if unavailable.
white a granulated, coarse table sugar, also known as crystal sugar.

SUGAR SNAP PEAS also known as honey snap peas; small, fresh pea that can be eaten, whole, pod and all, similarly to a snow peas.

SULTANAS dried grapes, also known as golden raisins.

TAHINI a rich sesame seed paste available from Middle-Eastern food stores; most often used in hummus, baba ghanoush and other Lebanese-style recipes.

TOMATOES
egg also called plum or roma, these are smallish, oval-shaped tomatoes.
paste triple-concentrated tomato puree used to flavour soups, stews, sauces and casseroles.
teardrop small yellow, pear-shaped tomatoes.
truss small vine-ripened tomatoes with the vine still attached.

TORTILLA thin, unleavened, round bread originating in Mexico; can be purchased frozen, vacuum-packed or fresh. Two kinds are available, one made from wheat and the other from corn.

TREACLE thick, dark syrup, not unlike molasses; a by-product of sugar refining.

VIETNAMESE MINT not a mint at all, but a pungent, peppery narrow-leafed member of the buckwheat family. Available from Asian food stores.

VINEGAR
balsamic authentic only from the province of Modena, Italy; made from a regional wine of white Trebbiano grapes specially processed then aged in antique wooden casks giving it an exquisite pungent flavour.
cider made from fermented apples.
red wine based on fermented red wine.
white wine made from white wine.

VINE LEAVES available in brine, jars and cryovac packs. Can be found in most Middle-Eastern food stores.

WATER CHESTNUTS look like chestnuts, hence the English name. They are small brown tubers with a crisp, white, nutty-tasting flesh.

WATERCRESS one of the cress family, a large group of peppery greens used raw in salads, dips and sandwiches, or cooked in soups. Highly perishable, so must be used as soon as possible after purchase.

WONTON WRAPPERS also known as wonton skins; made of flour, eggs and water, they come in varying thicknesses. Sold packaged in large amounts and found in the refrigerated section of supermarkets or Asian food stores.

ZUCCHINI also known as courgette; small green, yellow or white members of the squash family, having edible flowers.

CONVERSION CHART

MEASURES

One Australian metric measuring cup holds approximately 250ml; one Australian metric tablespoon holds 20ml; one Australian metric teaspoon holds 5ml.

The difference between one country's measuring cups and another's is within a two- or three-teaspoon variance, and will not affect your cooking results. North America, New Zealand and the United Kingdom use a 15ml tablespoon.

All cup and spoon measurements are level. The most accurate way of measuring dry ingredients is to weigh them. When measuring liquids, use a clear glass or plastic jug with the metric markings.

We use large eggs with an average weight of 60g.

DRY MEASURES

METRIC	IMPERIAL
15g	½oz
30g	1oz
60g	2oz
90g	3oz
125g	4oz (¼lb)
155g	5oz
185g	6oz
220g	7oz
250g	8oz (½lb)
280g	9oz
315g	10oz
345g	11oz
375g	12oz (¾lb)
410g	13oz
440g	14oz
470g	15oz
500g	16oz (1lb)
750g	24oz (1½lb)
1kg	32oz (2lb)

LIQUID MEASURES

METRIC	IMPERIAL
30ml	1 fluid oz
60ml	2 fluid oz
100ml	3 fluid oz
125ml	4 fluid oz
150ml	5 fluid oz (¼ pint/1 gill)
190ml	6 fluid oz
250ml	8 fluid oz
300ml	10 fluid oz (½ pint)
500ml	16 fluid oz
600ml	20 fluid oz (1 pint)
1000ml (1 litre)	1¾ pints

LENGTH MEASURES

METRIC	IMPERIAL
3mm	⅛in
6mm	¼in
1cm	½in
2cm	¾in
2.5cm	1in
5cm	2in
6cm	2½in
8cm	3in
10cm	4in
13cm	5in
15cm	6in
18cm	7in
20cm	8in
23cm	9in
25cm	10in
28cm	11in
30cm	12in (1ft)

OVEN TEMPERATURES

These oven temperatures are only a guide for conventional ovens. For fan-forced ovens, check the manufacturer's manual.

	°C (CELSIUS)	°F (FAHRENHEIT)	GAS MARK
Very slow	120	250	½
Slow	150	275-300	1-2
Moderately slow	160	325	3
Moderate	180	350-375	4-5
Moderately hot	200	400	6
Hot	220	425-450	7-8
Very hot	240	475	9

INDEX

ARE YOU MISSING SOME OF THE WORLD'S FAVOURITE COOKBOOKS?

The Australian Women's Weekly Cookbooks are available from bookshops, cookshops, supermarkets and other stores all over the world. You can also buy direct from the publisher, using the order form below.

TITLE	RRP	QTY	TITLE	RRP	QTY
Asian, Meals in Minutes	£6.99		Japanese Cooking Class	£6.99	
Babies & Toddlers Good Food	£6.99		Just For One (Feb 07)	£6.99	
Barbecue Meals In Minutes	£6.99		Kids' Birthday Cakes	£6.99	
Beginners Cooking Class	£6.99		Kids Cooking	£6.99	
Beginners Simple Meals	£6.99		Kids' Cooking Step-by-Step	£6.99	
Beginners Thai	£6.99		Lean Food	£6.99	
Best Food	£6.99		Low-carb, Low-fat	£6.99	
Best Food Desserts	£6.99		Low-fat Feasts	£6.99	
Best Food Fast	£6.99		Low-fat Food For Life	£6.99	
Best Food Mains	£6.99		Low-fat Meals in Minutes	£6.99	
Cafe Classics	£6.99		Main Course Salads	£6.99	
Cakes Biscuits & Slices	£6.99		Mexican	£6.99	
Cakes Cooking Class	£6.99		Middle Eastern Cooking Class	£6.99	
Caribbean Cooking	£6.99		Midweek Meals in Minutes	£6.99	
Casseroles	£6.99		Moroccan & and Foods of North Africa	£6.99	
Casseroles & Slow-Cooked Classics	£6.99		Muffins, Scones & Breads	£6.99	
Cheesecakes: baked and chilled	£6.99		New Casseroles	£6.99	
Chicken	£6.99		New Classics	£6.99	
Chicken Meals in Minutes	£6.99		New Curries	£6.99	
Chinese Cooking Class	£6.99		New Finger Food	£6.99	
Christmas Cooking	£6.99		New Salads	£6.99	
Chocolate	£6.99		Party Food and Drink	£6.99	
Cocktails	£6.99		Pasta Meals in Minutes	£6.99	
Cooking for Friends	£6.99		Potatoes	£6.99	
Cupcakes & Fairycakes	£6.99		Salads: Simple, Fast & Fresh	£6.99	
Detox	£6.99		Saucery	£6.99	
Dinner Beef	£6.99		Sauces Salsas & Dressings	£6.99	
Dinner Lamb	£6.99		Sensational Stir-Fries	£6.99	
Dinner Seafood	£6.99		Slim	£6.99	
Easy Australian Style	£6.99		Stir-fry	£6.99	
Easy Curry	£6.99		Superfoods for Exam Success	£6.99	
Easy Spanish-Style	£6.99		Sweet Old Fashioned Favourites	£6.99	
Essential Soup	£6.99		Tapas Mezze Antipasto & other bites	£6.99	
French Food, New	£6.99		Thai Cooking Class	£6.99	
Fresh Food for Babies & Toddlers	£6.99		Traditional Italian	£6.99	
Good Food Fast	£6.99		Vegetarian Meals in Minutes	£6.99	
Great Lamb Cookbook	£6.99		Vegie Food	£6.99	
Greek Cooking Class	£6.99		Wicked Sweet Indulgences	£6.99	
Grills	£6.99		Wok, Meals in Minutes	£6.99	
Healthy Heart Cookbook	£6.99				
Indian Cooking Class	£6.99		TOTAL COST:	£	

Mr/Mrs/Ms _____

Address _____

_____ Postcode _____

Day time phone _____ Email* (optional) _____

I enclose my cheque/money order for £ _____

or please charge £ _____

to my: ☐ Access ☐ Mastercard ☐ Visa ☐ Diners Club

PLEASE NOTE: WE DO NOT ACCEPT SWITCH OR ELECTRON CARDS

Card number ☐☐☐☐ ☐☐☐☐ ☐☐☐☐ ☐☐☐☐

Expiry date _____ 3 digit security code *(found on reverse of card)* _____

Cardholder's name_____ Signature _____

To order: Mail or fax – photocopy or complete the order form above, and send your credit card details or cheque payable to: Australian Consolidated Press (UK), Moulton Park Business Centre, Red House Road, Moulton Park, Northampton NN3 6AQ, phone (+44) (0) 1604 497531 fax (+44) (0) 1604 497533, e-mail books@acpmedia.co.uk or order online at www.acpuk.com
Non-UK residents: We accept the credit cards listed on the coupon, or cheques, drafts or International Money Orders payable in sterling and drawn on a UK bank. Credit card charges are at the exchange rate current at the time of payment.
Postage and packing UK: Add £1.00 per order plus 50p per book.
Postage and packing overseas: Add £2.00 per order plus £1.00 per book.
All pricing current at time of going to press and subject to change/availability.
Offer ends 31.12.2007

* By including your email address, you consent to receipt of any email regarding this magazine, and other emails which inform you of ACP's other publications, products, services and events, and to promote third party goods and services you may be interested in.